EARLY CHRISTIAN MYSTICS

THE DIVINE VISION OF
THE SPIRITUAL MASTERS

BERNARD MCGINN
AND
PATRICIA FERRIS MCGINN

A Crossroad Book
The Crossroad Publishing Company
New York

The Crossroad Publishing Company
481 Eighth Avenue, New York, NY 10001

Several portions of this book include revised and expanded material from *The Foundations of Mysticism* and *The Growth of Mysticism*, both by Bernard McGinn.

Illustrations by Bro. Michael O'Neill McGrath, OSFS

Printed in the United States of America

Library of Congress Cataloging-in-Publication Data

McGinn, Bernard, 1937–
    Early Christian mystics : the divine vision of the spiritual masters / Bernard McGinn and Patricia Ferris McGinn.
      p. cm.
    Includes bibliographical references.
    ISBN 0-8245-2106-4 (alk. paper)
    1. Mysticism – History – Early church, ca. 30--600. 2. Mysticism – History – Middle Ages, 600-1500. I. McGinn, Patricia Ferris. II. Title.
BV5075.M365 2003
248.2′2′09 – dc21

2003003726

1 2 3 4 5 6 7 8 9 10   10 09 08 07 06 05 04 03

In Memoriam
Katie and Jack Ferris

Contents

Introduction

Twelve, like three and seven, is one of the sacred numbers. Prominent in the Bible, it seems inscribed into the very cosmos, as its use in many religious traditions attests. Twelve often signifies sacred foundations in the human world. The twelve patriarchs stand at the origin of the Jewish people, just as the twelve apostles are the foundation upon which Christ built his church. Tradition and imagination have discerned numerous other twelves in sacred history, such as the twelve prophets of the Hebrew Bible and the twelve fruits of the Holy Spirit mentioned by Paul. The Calabrian seer Joachim of Fiore (d. 1202) was particularly fertile in discerning historical patterns of twelves, often by combining sevens and fives, as one of the keys to unlock the action of divine providence.

In putting together this brief introduction to the Christian mystical tradition up to the year 1200, it was no accident, though not originally a conscious choice, that the number twelve emerged as the most fitting for a selection of figures to illustrate the foundations of Christian mysticism. The dozen sketches contained here are based on the treatments found in the first two volumes of the ongoing series *The Presence of God: A History of Western Christian Mysticism.** While the portraits below are based on material from *The Presence of God*, they have been adapted for a more general

*Three volumes have appeared thus far: *The Foundations of Mysticism: Origins to the Fifth Century* (1991); *The Growth of Mysticism: Gregory the Great through the Twelfth Century* (1994); and *The Flowering of Mysticism: Men and Women in the New Mysticism — 1200–1350* (1998).

9

audience in numerous ways. Not only has the apparatus of footnotes and technical discussion been left behind, but we have sought to focus each portrait on a distinctive contribution that the mystic made to the broader tradition. This has led to the introduction of new material in some places and the rearrangement and recasting of the older material in others. While most of the sketches are necessarily shorter than the extended treatments in *The Presence of God*, in a few cases, such as Gregory of Nyssa and Hildegard of Bingen, they are actually longer. Like *The Presence of God*, *Early Christian Mystics* concentrates on Western Christian mysticism, so only those patristic Greek mystics are treated who had some significant impact on the West (Origen, Evagrius, Gregory of Nyssa, Dionysius). This means that some of the later Byzantine figures, notably Maximus Confessor (d. 662) and Symeon the New Theologian (d. 1022), will not be treated here, though they too are foundational for the wider story of Christian mysticism up to 1200.

The mystical element in Christianity, as we are using the term "mystical" here, is that part of belief and practice that concerns the preparation for, the consciousness of, and the reaction to what the mystics understand as a direct, immediate, and transformative encounter with the presence of God. Though many mystics speak of such transformative direct contact as attaining union with God, others avoid this language, so we have preferred to speak of presence. But presence itself, like so much else in mysticism, is not a simple and straightforward notion. God cannot be present the way a thing is present, because God is literally no-thing. God may become present in a way somehow similar to how two persons are present to each other, especially in the presence of lovers;

but God as infinite person so far exceeds the categories and consciousness characteristic of our own finite subjectivity that the divine presence is often realized in forms of absence and negation that mystics have explored with courage, tenacity, and great subtlety. One thing that all mystics insist upon is that what they come to know of God through their yearning for and meeting with the divine presence is incommunicable, at least insofar as we understand ordinary communication. As one of the pre-1200 mystics not treated here once said: "We say what we can when we want to speak about the Ineffable One about whom nothing can be said in the proper sense; we must either keep silence, or use words in a transformed way" (Isaac of Stella, Sermon 22). Conveying mystical consciousness is a necessary impossibility.

Despite the ambiguities of presence and absence, and notwithstanding the impossibility of really saying what they found, the transformation that the early Christian mystics underwent impelled them to speak and to write in order to invite others to undertake the path they walked. In trying to understand the different aspects of that search as it is presented by the twelve figures treated here, it is important to stress a few basic characteristics of mysticism that have not always been properly understood.

First, mysticism is an element in the Christian religion, not a religion within the religion. Each of the figures treated below was certainly a mystic but also an individual who lived in the midst of the Christian community, which each served in many other capacities, such as teacher, monastic, bishop, and even pope. To call them mystics does not exhaust their other activities and contributions to the history of Christianity.

Second, it is also important to see mysticism as a total process, not merely some particular moment or moments in or
beyond time where special contact with God is made. Mysticism is a journey, a path that almost invariably demands
long preparation and whose true attainment can be measured
only by the effects that mystics have upon others, both their
contemporaries and their readers over the centuries. All the
mystics took finding deeper contact with God as the central goal of their lives. The purpose of this volume is to make
some small contribution to the ongoing dissemination of their
transformative message.

Since Christian mystics live and teach in the midst of the
community with its many and changing beliefs and practices,
these twelve mystics have much to say about the Christian
life in general. Reading and praying the Bible, partaking of
the sacraments, practicing asceticism and self-denial, training
in virtue, devotion to higher forms of prayer and contemplation — these are all implied and often explicitly set forth
in the writings of these early mystics. Various attempts to
describe the deeper, more direct, and personally intimate
encounter with God that characterizes mystical consciousness are also expressed in a wide variety of ways among the
writings of the mystics.

In the sketches below we have tried to give a sense of the
general teaching of each figure, but we have also sought to
highlight one distinctive aspect of the thought that characterizes each mystic's contribution to the broader tradition.
Mystical writers over the centuries have used a variety of
styles, voices, and teaching methods. Each of the chapters
that follow tries to suggest this by centering on a special

contribution that demonstrates how the figure treated can be considered a true founder of mysticism.

We have divided the twelve chapters into two sections, each chronologically arranged, to reflect these different forms of contribution. Part One concentrates on *Practices for Finding God*. It begins with the Alexandrian catechist and preacher Origen (d. 253), the greatest exegete of the early church. The theologian Hans Urs von Balthasar once said that no figure is more invisibly all-present in the history of Christianity than Origen. Given the immense influence of his spiritual and "anagogic," or uplifting, reading of the Bible, chapter 1 highlights this theme in Origen's thought. A fourth-century monastic follower of Origen, Evagrius Ponticus (d. 399), took Origen's basic theology of the soul's return to God and wedded it to the new form of religious life created by the monks and nuns of the Egyptian desert with their devotion to rigorous asceticism and a life of contemplation. His teaching on these subjects is taken up in chapter 2. Evagrius's mystical teaching was conveyed to the Latin West by another monk, John Cassian (d. 435), who founded some of the earliest monastic communities in Gaul. Cassian, however, was not merely a conduit; he was an original practitioner and teacher of mysticism. Cassian's doctrine on the modes of prayer, and especially on the necessity for attaining purity of heart in order to reach God, is the subject of chapter 3. The mystical teaching of Pope Gregory the Great (d. 604) is treated in chapter 4. Gregory's solidly biblical doctrine touches on many aspects of mysticism, but we have concentrated on the theme of compunction, "being pierced to the heart," both through sorrow for sin and in mystical love of God, as his central contribution.

Hildegard of Bingen (d. 1179), a Benedictine nun, was arguably the most multitalented figure of her remarkable age. Hildegard was interested in science and medicine; she was a gifted poet and musician, a dramatist and artist, and an original theologian. Hildegard was also a mystic, and chapter 5 shows how her mysticism and teaching authority were rooted in some of the extraordinary visions she received. Chapter 6 treats Richard of St. Victor (d. 1173), a canon, that is, a priest and teacher living according to a monasticized form of life. Richard's importance lies in the fact that with him we see the coming together of the wisdom of monastic mysticism with the new organizing and systematizing form of the theology found in early scholasticism. Building on the work of his teacher, Hugh of St. Victor (d. 1141), Richard organized progress in attaining virtues and the ascending modes of contemplation into an integrated mystical teaching that was to be influential for many centuries.

Part Two considers the ways in which early Christian mystics sought to characterize essential aspects of transformative contact with God. Gregory of Nyssa (d. 394) is one of the three great Cappadocian Fathers whose teachings formed early Orthodox Christianity. Gregory was also a profound and passionate mystical seeker. His sense of the absolute infinity and unsurpassability of God led him to formulate a teaching on the endless pursuit of God, both in this life and in the hereafter, as the essence of mystical transformation. This is treated in chapter 7. Christians have always believed that attaining God is possible only in and through Jesus Christ. Christ is the goal and Christ is the way, especially the whole Christ, that is, Christ as head and as body, the church. The ecclesiological character of mysticism is set out by virtually all early mystics, but by none in a deeper and more convincing way than by Augustine of Hippo (d. 430), who is the subject of chapter 8. Chapter 9 considers the mysterious Dionysius, an Eastern monk influenced both by the Cappadocians and by Greek pagan Neoplatonists, who wrote around 500 C.E. Adopting the guise of Dionysius the Areopagite mentioned in Acts 17:34, this anonymous writer was the first to use the term "mystical theology" to describe the aim of a liturgically centered Christian life dedicated to uniting with God as the mystery beyond all knowing. While earlier Christian mystics often spoke of how God lies beyond all that we can know and say, Dionysius was the first to put forth an integrated and systematic negative, or "apophatic," mysticism of unknowing knowing.

In passing to the medieval section of Part Two, chapter 10 deals with the Irish writer Johannes Scottus Eriugena, or John the Scot (d. ca. 880), a teacher at the courts of the descendants of Charlemagne. Eriugena has justly been seen as the greatest philosopher and theologian of the early medieval West, and we argue that he is also a great mystic. Eriugena sought to forge a consensus between the authorities of the East (Gregory of Nyssa, Dionysius, Maximus Confessor) and the West (Augustine, Ambrose, and others). To do so he set forth a systematic understanding of the dynamism of *natura*, that is, God both as hidden in himself (the apophatic aspect) and as manifest in the theophany of his creation (the positive, or "cataphatic," aspect). Building upon Dionysius (whom he translated into Latin), Eriugena created a cosmic mysticism rooted in humanity and Christ, the Godman.

The final two chapters deal with twelfth-century mystics. Bernard of Clairvaux (d. 1153) is rightly considered the touchstone of Western mysticism. When Dante needed someone to introduce the trinitarian vision of God that concludes the *Paradiso*, he could think of no more appropriate figure than this Cistercian monk. Bernard's *Sermons on the Song of Songs*, eighty-six masterly homilies on the first three chapters of the Song as the mystery of love between the human soul, the bride, and Christ, the Bridegroom, are among the most influential of all mystical texts. Bernard's mysticism of spousal love is examined in chapter 11. Bernard's close friend William of St. Thierry (d. 1147), a Benedictine abbot turned Cistercian monk, also wrote a commentary on the Song, as well as a number of mystical treatises. His noted work *The Golden Letter*, the most incisive brief portrayal of monastic mysticism, often circulated under Bernard's name in later centuries. William was an original mystic, however, not a mere student of his friend. This is especially evident in his profound teaching about the role of the Trinity in the mystical life, the subject of chapter 12.

A brief note about the genesis of this book is in order. Over several years the staff at the Crossroad Publishing Company, beginning with Michael Leach (now of Orbis Books) and continuing with Gwendolin Herder and John Jones, had asked Bernard McGinn to consider preparing a short popular account of early Christian mystics based on *The Presence of God* volumes. The pressure of research and writing for the later volumes of the series, as well as other obligations, seemed to preclude producing such a book. It was only in early 2002 that we realized that if we were to undertake the volume as a joint project, it might, indeed, be possible. Patricia Ferris McGinn had contributed much to the already-published volumes of *The Presence of God* through her editing and suggestions. Knowing the volumes as well as she did, she took up the initial task of summarizing and adapting most of the chapters from the longer treatments in *The Presence of God.* Each of these sketches then was reworked as a joint effort. Finally, Bernard McGinn added the "Suggestions for Further Reading" found after each sketch. These are meant to serve as brief introductions to translations of the writings of the mystics. A few helpful monographs are listed as well. More complete bibliographies can be found in *The Presence of God.*

We want to thank our family, especially Daniel, John, and Gina, and all our friends, both at Crossroad and elsewhere, who have encouraged us as we pursued this collaboration with love and joy.

BERNARD McGINN AND
PATRICIA FERRIS McGINN
December 2002

Part One

PRACTICES
FOR FINDING GOD

One

Uplifting Reading of Scripture

ORIGEN

LIFE

It was 202 in Alexandria. The mother was frantic with grief and fear, and when her entreaties did not deter him, she hid her eldest son's clothes so he could not leave the house. Her husband, Leonides, had been arrested and would be beheaded as a Christian martyr during the persecution of the emperor Septimius Severus, and her son Origen was burning with desire to follow his father into martyrdom. Her tactic worked, however, and Origen, seventeen years old, lived to support his mother and his six younger brothers by teaching "grammar" (that is, literature). His father had seen to it that he had both an excellent secular education and a deep indoctrination into the study of the scriptures.

Eusebius, the historian of the early church, says that all of the Christian catechists had left Alexandria during the persecution, so when pagans came to him for instruction, Origen took up the additional role of elementary teacher of the Christian faith. By age eighteen he was head of the school of catechesis for the church of Alexandria. Eusebius credits him with bringing thousands into the Christian faith, and he was known for his courage in accompanying martyrs to their public executions despite the fury of the pagan crowds. Later he relinquished secular teaching, sold his library to raise money to live on, and focused solely on the roles of cate- chist, preacher, student of scripture, and ascetic (or Christian philosopher), roles in which he became very famous.

Origen is famous also for his self-castration, as we are told by Eusebius. This action has remained mysterious and controversial: it seems to have been the result of an overly zealous young man taking Matthew 19:12 literally ("There are those who have made themselves eunuchs for the sake of the kingdom of heaven"), despite the fact that church tra- dition, even then, understood the passage allegorically. His condition, however, did make it easier for him to teach and preach to women without scandal.

Origen's growing fame led to trips abroad. His ordination to presbyter in Palestine caused a break with Demetrius, the bishop of Alexandria, after which Origen relocated to Cae- sarea in 233 to continue his work of teaching, preaching, and writing. Though he was arrested and tortured in the persecution of emperor Decius in 250, martyrdom still eluded him, and he died in 253 or 254.

INTERPRETING THE SCRIPTURES AS A SPIRITUAL PATH

We have only a portion of Origen's vast literary output, but these works show him to combine the roles of exegete, theologian, and mystic with great creativity and intellectual power. While these three modes of thought are intimately related in his work, Origen remains first and foremost an exegete, perhaps the greatest that Christianity has ever known. It is in his *Commentary on John* and *Commentary and Homilies on the Song of Songs* that we find the chief elements of his mystical thought. The most important work for grasping the main features of his "theology of ascent," as Hans Urs von Balthasar described it, is *On First Principles (De principiis)*, the earliest Christian systematic theology.

As a product of the philosophical education of his time and yet as a Christian, Origen understood the true "philosophy," the love of wisdom and the truth about the self sought by Plato and the Greeks, to be found not in contemplation of the heavens and the study of human society, but in the revealed scriptures. For him scripture in its entirety is nothing else than the Logos, or Word of God, teaching each believer in and through the church. The Logos eternally begotten from the Father's self-emptying, who in turn emptied himself by taking on flesh, now becomes present and active in us through the mediation of his presence in the inspired words of the scripture. The intimate relation between reading the scriptures and reading the self (and, by extension, knowing how to read the cosmos) is brought out in a well-known passage in the fourth book of *On First Principles:*

> One must therefore portray the meaning of the sacred writings in a threefold way upon one's own soul, so that the simple man may be edified by what we may call the flesh of scripture . . . , while the man who has made some progress may be edified by its soul, as it were; and the man who is perfect . . . may be edified by the spiritual law. . . . For just as a man consists of body, soul, and spirit, so in the same way does the scripture, which has been prepared by God to be given for man's salvation. (4.2.4)

Following the formula of St. Paul, Origen thus identifies three levels in the human person — body, soul, and spirit — and sees the true relation of these three components realized through personal appropriation of the scriptural message at three levels. The encounter with the text provides the spiritual education by which we reach for the true goal of life.

The first level consists in determining the literal sense of the biblical text. Here Origen was conscious of a twofold task: first, grasping the grammatical sense of the words and, second, discovering the historical reality of the passage. At times a passage is not to be taken literally, meaning that it could not or did not happen historically (see *On First Principles* 4.2.5), but that does not diminish the fact that the grammatical meaning of the words carries a deeper message for believers.

Still Origen, following Paul, taught the necessity of moving beyond the "letter that kills" to the second level (corresponding to the soul) for the moral meaning and the third level (corresponding to the spirit) for the mystical meaning of the scriptures. These moral and spiritual teachings of the Logos are discerned through a variety of allegorical and typological tools applied to the text. In the New Testament the teaching of the Logos is direct, while in the Old Testament the teaching is mediated through others as the events and persons of the Old Testament come to be understood as "types" and "allegories" of present realities. Though allegorical and typological exegesis is part of Origen's heritage from both the Jewish and the Hellenic past, he is the first Christian to describe the personal appropriation of the teaching of the Logos as an "anagogic" reading, one designed to lift the soul above. "The scribe of the gospel is one who knows how, after studying the narrative of events, to ascend to the spiritual realities without stumbling" (*Commentary on Matthew* 10.14). The goal of interpretation is to realize the Bible's teaching through our own ascension to God, a process that Origen once expressed as wishing "to gallop through the vast spaces of mystic and spiritual understanding" (*Commentary on Romans* 7.11). Through the encounter with the scriptures, using the tools of spiritual interpretation, the soul ascends back to its source in God. For Origen, this journey of ascent is the essence of the Christian vocation and the main motif of his mysticism.

Christian Platonist that he was, Origen needed to posit a descent from God as a prior condition to explain the necessity of the ascent of the soul back to God. Creation, the extradivine manifestation of the goodness of the Father, first becomes manifest in the Logos. In the Logos the ideas or causes, which are the prototypes for everything that comes to be in the actual universe, exist from all eternity. The Logos is both the model of creation and the intelligent agent through which the Father produces it. On the basis of these causes, God creates the intelligible universe, a prior and perfect creation whose fall made necessary the second creation. This second creation is the world of division, hierarchy, and sin that we inhabit. In his first Homily on Genesis, Origen asserts "... that first heaven, which we said is spiritual, is our mind, which is also itself spirit, that is, our spiritual man which sees and perceives God" (*Hom. on Gen.* 1.2). The original spiritual creation was composed of "intellects" all created equal after the pattern of the only true Image, the Logos (*Hom. on Gen.* 1.12–13). This is the creation described in the first chapter of Genesis. These intellects, each guided by a *pneuma,* or participation in the Holy Spirit, were joined to spiritual bodies and lived a joyous life of contemplation of God, "a pure and perfect reception of God into itself" (*On First Principles* 4.4.9). Together they constituted the supreme unity of the preexistent church under the headship of the one intellect, perfectly united in love with the Logos, that is, the intellect of the preexistent Christ.

The fundamental characteristic of these intellects, however, was the freedom given to them by God — divine goodness and the freedom of spiritual creation are the lynchpins of Origen's thought. It was this freedom that made possible the original fall from perfect contemplation:

For the Creator granted to the minds created by him the power of free and voluntary movement, in order that

the good that was in them might become their own,
since it was preserved by their own free will. But sloth
and weariness of taking trouble to preserve the good,
coupled with disregard and neglect of better things,
began the process of withdrawal from the good. (*On
First Principles* 2.9.2)

Diversity and evil in our present world measure the degree of
the fall from perfect contemplation without denigrating the
Creator's goodness. Humans are intellects who fell further
than the angels and were provided a second, material creation as the schoolroom in which to work out their destinies.
Material creation is more an educational opportunity than a
punishment, since matter, including the human body, is not
evil but part of God's good creation, a limited good whose
real purpose is to teach intellects to ascend above it in their
path back to unimpeded vision of God.

---

*"We believe that the goodness of God through
Christ will restore his entire creation to one end,
even his enemies being conquered and subdued."*
—Origen, *On First Principles*

The fallen intellects constitute the core of the human person, composed of the three levels with which we are familiar:
(1) *pneuma*, or spirit, the created participation in the Holy
Spirit, which has become inert in fallen humanity; (2) *pysche*,
or soul, which is the "cooled" state of intellect in the fallen
condition, able either to be redirected above to contemplation of God through the instruction of spirit, or else dragged

below by the sensuality to the level of (3) *soma,* the body, humanity's material component. Because each intellect was created as a participation in the Logos, it remains capable of regaining its original state of contemplative likeness to God through the pedagogic activity of the Logos, the Word who takes on flesh in Jesus Christ through the mediation of the one unfallen intellect, the soul of Christ. Through Jesus' unfailing love and unbroken contemplation of God, his soul becomes the model and teacher for all other souls as they awaken the *pneuma* within themselves and begin to return to God. Origen said, "We believe that the goodness of God through Christ will restore his entire creation to one end, even his enemies being conquered and subdued" (*On First Principles* 1.6.1). This insight, which Origen found expressed in Paul's words that in the end God will be "all in all" (1 Cor. 15:28), is fundamental to his mysticism, though the idea that the demons might be included creates serious problems for later Christian orthodoxy.

For Origen the whole message of scripture concerns the descent and ascent of the Incarnate Word to rescue the fallen intellects. All other metaphors he uses are subservient to this itinerary: the passage upward to God achieved by and in Christ. The difficult and wandering journey by which the soul returns to God begins from the clear "bread" of direct scriptural language but can advance only through ingestion of the "wine" of scripture, its obscure and poetic speech, which intoxicates and draws one upward. Thus, for the Alexandrian, the spiritual life is an exegetical process in which religious experience, especially mystical experience, is realized in the act of making the language of the Bible at its deepest and incommunicable level into the soul's language.

Origen's most intense religious experiences took place within the work of exegesis itself; this is where the soul rises with the Incarnate Word.

Origen presents the soul's exegetical-mystical ascent according to a basic triple pattern of pedagogy found in the three books ascribed to Solomon. The itinerary is as follows:

1. Proverbs teaches what the Greeks call moral science, the proper manner of virtuous living that corresponds to the life of the patriarch Abraham and to what later Christians would call the "purgative" way.

2. Ecclesiastes presents natural science, that is, enlightened knowledge of the natures of things and of how they are to be used as God intended (corresponding to Isaac and the "illuminative" way).

3. Finally, the Song of Songs is the textbook for what Origen calls *epoptics,* the contemplative science that "instills love and desire of celestial and divine things under the image of the Bride and the Groom, teaching how we come to fellowship with God through paths of love and charity" (*Commentary on the Song,* prol.). When the soul has completed the first two courses of study, "it is ready to come to dogmatic and mystical matters and to arise to the contemplation of divinity with pure spiritual love" (ibid). This is the science of Jacob, who became Israel ("he who sees God"). It forms the "unitive," or properly mystical, level.

The essential message from the Alexandrian is that "the true food of a rational nature is the Word of God" (*Homilies on Numbers* 27.1). The goal of human life, according to Origen, is the light and abundance of the Promised Land. Both in teaching and in temperament Origen concentrates on the positive rather than the negative, or apophatic, aspects of the enjoyment of God's presence. He is rightly characterized as a "mystic of light."

As the Alexandrian teacher develops the theme of the soul's return to God, he uses many symbols and images drawn from the Bible, but it is in the Song of Songs that scripture reveals the heart of its message about the love of the descending Christ for the fallen soul. In the interpretation of the erotic language of the Song the deepest inscription of the mystical message takes place. Origen stands at the head of those Christian mystics who have argued that of all the positive, or cataphatic, modes of speaking available to the mystic, erotic language is the most appropriate way of using speech to surpass itself. Contrary to some modern critiques, the mystics have always insisted that they were neither disguising nor idealizing eros, but rather that they were transforming desire by leading it back to its original form: eros is in reality a heavenly force. "The power of love is none other than that which leads the soul from earth to the lofty heights of heaven, and . . . the highest beatitude can be attained only under the stimulus of love's desire" (*Comm. on Song,* prol.). Adapting Plato's teaching that eros is a desire to attain what is perfect and to beget from this attainment, Origen makes a daring breakthrough — God himself must be Eros if the eros implanted in us is what returns us to him. He says, "I do not think one could be blamed if one called God Passionate Love (*eros/amor*), just as John calls him Charity (*agapē/ caritas*)" (*Comm. on Song,* prol.). Therefore, "you must take whatever scripture says about charity (*caritas*) as if it had been

said in reference to passionate love (*amor*), taking no notice
of the difference in terms; for the same meaning is conveyed
by both" (ibid.).

Origen took the notion of God as Eros with great seri-
ousness. Few ancient thinkers have more clearly expressed
the tension between the realization of God's yearning for the
world and the power of the notion of the absolute unchange-
ability of the Ultimate. "God so loved the world" (John 3:16)
was not a mere metaphor for Origen. In a few texts he dares
to assert a kind of "suffering" in God, and some Origen scholars have argued that the "passion of the Word" in emptying
himself to take on flesh is one of Origen's most profound
theological insights.

If, as Origen believed, eros has its source above and has
been implanted in us by God-Eros (we could call this EROS I),
the motive force powering the soul's ascent must be the
transformation of the eros gone awry in us (EROS II) back
to its transcendental starting place. Origen's *Commentary
on the Song of Songs* contains the first Christian theoretical
exposition of this transformation.

Origen begins by insisting that EROS II can be transformed only by turning it away from the inferior material
and human objects to which it has become directed in its
fallen state. Hence, any form of erotic practice, especially
sexual love (even that legitimately allowed by the church),
is irrelevant (or more likely harmful) for the transformative
process. Origen's emphasis on the privileged role of virginity as the manifestation of the soul's preexisting purity and
God-directed freedom marks the earliest theoretical defense
in Christianity of the strict division between sexual practice

and mystical endeavor. It has also been one of the distinctive marks of much, though not all, Christian mysticism.

Origen bases this disjunction on the identification of Paul's notion of the inner and the outer person (e.g., 2 Cor. 4:16), that is, the flesh and the spirit, with the two creations. The inner person is the one created "in the image and likeness of God" (Gen. 1:26); the outer is that "formed from the slime of the earth" (Gen. 2:7). All the objects of desire characteristic of EROS II, from money and sexual pleasure to human arts and learning, are transitory and unworthy of true eros. The only true goal of eros is the spiritual good of the first creation, the manifestation of EROS I: "By that which is good we understand not anything corporeal, but only that which is found first in God and in the powers of the soul — it follows that the only laudable love is that which is directed to God and to the powers of the soul" (*Comm. on Song*, prol.).

But how exactly does the spiritual person learn to read the inner text behind the erotic images and longing language of the lovers in the Song of Songs? Here Origen bridges the gap between the inner and the outer person, between heavenly and carnal love, by means of the teaching about the spiritual senses of the soul that he developed from Clement of Alexandria. This is one of his most important contributions to the history of Christian mysticism.

According to the Alexandrian, "The divine scriptures make use of homonyms, that is to say, they use identical terms for describing different things . . . so that you will find the names of the members of the body transferred to those of the soul; or rather the faculties and powers of the soul are to be called its members" (*Comm. on Song*, prol.). Therefore, any bodily description contained in the Bible (and what book of scripture has more potent descriptions of body parts and bodily activities than the Song?) is actually a message about the inner person's relation to the Word because this person possesses "spiritual senses" analogous to the senses of taste, touch, hearing, smell, and sight by which the outer person relates to the material world. When one seeks the proper understanding of the erotic language of the Song, these higher and finer "senses" of the fallen, dormant intellect are awakened and resensitized by the spirit and made capable of receiving the transcendental experience of the presence of the Word. Origen calls this "a sensuality which has nothing sensual in it," as the language of the Song becomes the best way to read the inner text of the soul, and the spiritual senses guide the soul's mystical transformation.

As an example, we can take his interpretation of the famous opening verse of the Song, "Let him kiss me with the kisses of his mouth." Origen takes this erotic image through five levels of interpretation, which are both ecclesial and personal: (1) from the grammatical citation of the text and (2) its dramatic or historical reconstruction to (3) the deeper meanings of what it has to say about Christ's relation to the church, (4) its general message about the soul's itinerary, and finally (5) how we appropriate the message as our own. In summary, the message is that the sensation of receiving kisses is to be read as the mind's reception of the teaching of the Word, conveyed both to the church and to the individual soul. "When her mind is filled with divine perception and understanding without the agency of human or angelic ministration, then she may believe that she has received the kisses of the Word of God himself" (*Comm. on Song,* book 1).

Origen's reading of the image of the wound of love is more complex. He put together two texts, Isaiah 49:2 ("He set me as a chosen arrow") and Song of Songs 2:5 ("I am wounded with *agape*"), to create a rich and original teaching about the Word as the arrow or dart of the Father, whose love wounds the soul (the surviving texts all have an individual, not an ecclesial, application). In the Song commentary this appears with a personal and poignant tone in which the desire for the Word's teaching is expressed as a transcendental erotic obsession:

> If there is anyone anywhere who has at some time burned with this faithful love of the Word of God; if there is anyone who has at some time received the sweet wound of him who is the chosen dart, as the prophet says; if there is anyone who has been pierced with the loveworthy spear of his knowledge, so that he yearns and longs for him by day and night, can speak of naught but him, would hear of naught but him, can think of nothing else, and is disposed to no desire nor longing nor yet hope, except for him alone — if such there be, that soul then says in truth: "I have been wounded by charity." (*Comm. on Song*, book 3)

In passages such as these the spiritual sense of touch brings out a dimension of personal urgency not always found in relation to the other spiritual senses. There are some passages where Origen breaks through the calm web of his didactic tone with expressions of his own longing for the coming of the Word. In Homily 1.2, for example, he applies the embrace of the right and left hands of the Groom (Song 2:6) to the individual soul in a personal way: "For there is a certain spiritual embrace, and O that the Bridegroom's more perfect embrace may enfold my Bride!" Perhaps the most noted passage in the homilies, one of the few places where he speaks directly of himself, is a description, both exegetical and personal, combining the senses of spiritual seeing and touching:

> God is my witness that I have often perceived the Bridegroom drawing near me and being most intensely present with me; then suddenly he has withdrawn and I could not find him though I sought to do so. I long, therefore, for him to come again and sometimes he does so. Then, when he has appeared and I lay hold of him, he slips away once more; and when he has so slipped away, my search for him begins anew. (*Hom. on Song* 1:7)

Clearly, Origen is speaking in a voice that is at once that of the Bride in the text and his own. Although he uses the full range of the erotic images of the Song of Songs to describe how the spiritual senses contact the Divine Lover, spiritual "touch" and spiritual "vision" have a certain priority and seem to communicate a more intimate connection.

OTHER ASPECTS OF ORIGEN'S MYSTICISM

Good Greek that he was, Origen always conceived of the goal of the soul's journey in terms of knowledge, the higher knowledge and mystical vision of the mystery of Christ. Considerable disagreement exists, however, about whether this knowing is best described in "intellectual" or in "affective" terms. For Origen, this knowledge involves a personal relation to Jesus, and the intimacy of the union is suggested not only by the dominant image of the Bride and Groom, but also by the procreative symbol of birthing. Thus he can speak of the loving soul as both bride and mother: "And every soul, virgin and uncorrupted, which conceives by the Holy Spirit, so as to give birth to the Will of the Father, is the Mother of Jesus (*Comm. on Matt.*, Frg. 281). Thus, Origen's mystical form of knowing is primarily intellectual, but it is also affective, in part, a possession of the truth that satisfies both the noetic and the erotic dynamism of the soul. As the prologue to the *Commentary on the Song* puts it: "After realizing the beauty of the divine Word, we can allow ourselves to be set on fire with saving love, so that the Word itself deigns to love the soul in which it has encountered longing for it."

It is with a deep sense of joyful discovery that we can open ourselves to read the Bible with Origen's sense of the spiritual meaning of the text.

Origen was also the first to make the order of charity an important element in theological speculation. "Set charity in order in me" (Song 2:4b), the Bride asks of the friends of the Groom. Learning the degrees of charity — loving the proper objects in the right way — means loving God without measure, loving our neighbors as ourselves according to their role in Christ's body, loving enemies (though not as ourselves); in short, ordering all human affections according to the truth of the scriptures.

In discussing the relation of action to contemplation Origen found a Gospel basis for the superiority of contemplation in the account of Jesus' visit to Bethany (Luke 10:38–42), where the Savior praises Mary, representing the contemplative life, over Martha, the type of the active life. He does insist, however, that both modes must work together in shaping the soul. If the original state of the unfallen intellects was one of perfect contemplation of the Father, the very structure of creation confirms the superiority of the contemplative over the active life. In terms of the soul's itinerary, the purgative and illuminative stages represent the necessary activity that leads to the state of harmonious internal balance that overcomes the unruly passions. This makes it possible for the soul to live, as far as possible in this life, on the contemplative or theoretical level of *epoptics*.

The Alexandrian teacher emphasizes that the Father cannot be seen, but the Word, as the Father's perfect Image, both knows him and is known by him (Matt. 11:27). Hence, the Word made flesh becomes the "cleft in the rock" of Moses' vision (Exod. 33:21–23) in which we can come to know, that is, to "see" God with the heart, the interior sense of vision, as the beatitude promises: "Blessed are the pure of heart for they shall see God" (Matt. 5:8). Christ is the only way by which we can gain access to this vision: he is our guide to the delights of "mystical and ineffable contemplation" (*Commentary on John* 13.24). The vision begins in this life but will be completed only in the universal restoration when the intellect "will think God and see God and hold God and God will be the mode and measure of its every movement" (*On First Principles* 3.6.3).

What is the goal of Origen's understanding of anagogic, or uplifting, reading of the Bible? Like later mystics, Origen describes this goal in various ways. Essentially speaking, exegesis and contemplation lead to divinization of the soul. Origen underlines the distinctive character of Christian divinization as follows:

> For Christians see that with Jesus human and divine nature begin to be woven together, so that by fellowship with divinity human nature might become divine, not only in Jesus, but also in all those who believe and go on to undertake the life which Jesus taught, the life which leads everyone who lives according to Jesus' commandments to friendship with God and fellowship with Jesus. (*Against Celsus* 3.28)

Language of union (though not the modern term "mystical union") is also fairly frequent in Origen's writings. His understanding of union, based on his view of the distinction between Creator and creature, is always modeled on that of the lovers in the Song of Songs. Hence he often invokes the passage from 1 Corinthians 6:17 about becoming one spirit with God that would become the classic proof text for the loving union of hearts and minds to the exclusion of any union of identity or indistinction. Commenting on Song of Songs 2:10–13, he says: "For the Word of God would not otherwise say that she was his neighbor, did he not join himself to her and become one spirit with her" (*Comm. on Song,* book 3). For Origen this divinizing union was the fruit of the uplifting reading of scripture.

CONCLUSION

Though we do not live in the intellectual and spiritual world that formed Origen, we are not left with a merely intellectual and historical appreciation of his thought. Reading Origen challenges us — without setting aside our formation in the historical-critical approach to scripture — to approach the Song of Songs with an appreciation of the power of this erotic text to evoke the deepest yearnings of the believer for intimate contact with the Divine Lover. Contemporary Christians are no less fervent than those of Origen's time in their longing for God, and, despite our post-Freudian mentality, it is with a deep sense of joyful discovery that we can open ourselves to read the Bible with Origen's sense of the spiritual meaning of the text. We too can experience the reading and interpreting of scripture as a practice for finding God.

SUGGESTED FURTHER READING

Origen's greatest mystical work exists in a good English version: Origen, *The Song of Songs: Commentary and Homilies,* translated by R. P. Lawson, Ancient Christian Writers 26 (New York: Paulist Press, 1957). Origen's *On First Principles* has been translated by G. W. Butterworth (New York: Harper & Row, 1966). A number of the Alexandrian's spiritual writings can be found in Origen, *An Exhortation to Martyrdom* [and selected works], translated by Rowan Greer, Classics of Western Spirituality (New York: Paulist Press, 1979). Recently, the Fathers of the Church Series published by the Catholic University of America Press has made available good translations of many of Origen's homilies. An excellent collection of Origen's spiritual writings can be found in *Origen, Spirit and Fire: A Thematic Anthology of His Writings,* edited by Hans Urs von Balthasar (Washington, D.C.: Catholic University of America Press, 1984). For introductions to

Origen's thought, see Henri Crouzel, *Origen: The Life and Thought of the First Great Theologian* (San Francisco: Harper & Row, 1989); and Joseph W. Trigg, *Origen: The Bible and Philosophy in the Third-Century Church* (Atlanta: John Knox, 1983). For Origen's exegesis, see Karen Jo Torjesen, *Hermeneutical Procedure and Theological Method in Origen's Exegesis* (Berlin: Walter de Gruyter, 1986).

Two

Ascetical Practice and Contemplative Life

EVAGRIUS PONTICUS

LIFE

The brilliant deacon was in crisis. Having made a name for himself in the struggle for the Nicene faith against the Arians at the Second Ecumenical Council in 381, he was enjoying the intellectual and worldly life of Constantinople, the imperial capital. Evagrius of Pontus had received an excellent philosophical and theological education from Basil the Great and Gregory Nazianzus before being chosen as archdeacon by the bishop of Constantinople. But this important churchman had fallen in love with the wife of a high imperial official. To his dismay, he found he was losing the battle to control his passions. One night he had a dream in which he was accused in court of a vague crime he had not committed and for which he was going to be punished, and — still dreaming — he swore an oath to leave the city and tend to his soul. Two days later he was on his way to Jerusalem.

On the Mount of Olives Melania welcomed him. She was a wealthy Roman widow who had founded a convent as part of a double monastery with St. Jerome's former friend, Rufinus. Evagrius had a special gift for attracting the friendship and loyalty of serious, intellectual Christians, and Melania and Rufinus made him very comfortable — so comfortable, in fact, that he began again to get entangled in worldly ways. He contracted a fever that no medical attention could cure. With Melania's help he began to realize that this illness was about his broken promise to devote himself to the welfare of his soul, so, following her advice, he decided to join the "solitary ones," the monks in the Egyptian desert. Soon after, his fever abated. The relationship with Rufinus and Melania and later with the desert monks brought Evagrius in close contact with the teachings of Origen, which became the basis for his own thinking and teaching for the rest of his life.

Evagrius emerged as a leader among the desert monks. Later he moved deeper into the desert to join the more austere hermits at Cells, becoming a disciple of Macarius the Alexandrian and Macarius the Great. In addition to the difficulties a cultured Greek intellectual experienced in adapting to the physical rigors of desert life, the once-worldly deacon also had to make his way among the less educated Coptic peasants who were his fellow monks. In time, however, Evagrius learned the desert lessons of humility and silence, and he became known for his life of prayer and heroic ascetical practices. (One striking practice was to stand in a well through a winter's night to combat lustful thoughts.) Gifted with special talents for the discernment of spirits and with the loving personality that had always drawn people to him, he became much sought after as a spiritual master and guide. He lived at Cells for fourteen years until his premature death in 399 on the Feast of the Epiphany. He was fifty-five years old.

By the end of that year the followers of the Pontic master were being savagely persecuted as heretics for holding to the teachings of Origen. An even more severe condemnation of Origen, as well as of Evagrius himself, issued from the emperor Justinian in 543 and was included in an official anathema by the Second Ecumenical Council of Constantinople ten years later. Many of Evagrius's manuscripts were destroyed or preserved under other more respectable names. Though he is one of the major figures in the history of Christian mysticism, the whiff of heresy has hovered around him ever since.

EVAGRIUS AS ABBA AND WRITER

Disciples of the desert monks would seek out the abba, or spiritual father, for a word of salvation. A father was one whose life embodied the scriptures, a living testament. The most important role of the abba was to give the inquiring monk insight into the meaning of a biblical text and how he could apply it to his life circumstances — how the Word of God could change him and save him. Evagrius seems to have been the first of the desert fathers to shape these oral transmissions into literary form. Collections of his proverbs, even when not attributed to him, have provided guidance in the spiritual life ever since.

Abba Evagrius shows a wonderful understanding of the workings of the human heart in his proverbs directed to monks (the *Ad Monachos*). Here are some examples of Evagrius's practical advice for seekers:

> A strong wind chases away clouds;
> memory of injury chases the mind from knowledge.
>
> (no. 13)

> He who prays for his enemies will be forgetful of
>   injuries;
> he who spares his tongue will not sadden his neighbor.
>
> (no. 14)

> If your brother irritates you,
> lead him into your house,
> and do not hesitate to go into his,
> but eat your morsel with him.
> For doing this, you will deliver your soul
> and there will be no stumbling block for
> you at the hour of prayer. (no. 15)

The subtle development found in the proverbs of the *Ad Monachos* leads one who studies it deeply to understand the process of spiritual growth Evagrius sets out for monks. First, there is the ascetical work of freeing the soul from vices and acquiring virtues to reach the stage of spiritual and emotional tranquility called passionlessness (*apatheia*). This produces love, which leads to contemplation. Contemplation yields knowledge of the true nature of created things and of scripture, and further progress in contemplation brings one ultimately to the knowledge of God as the Holy Trinity. Again, Evagrius expresses this teaching in brief axioms:

> In front of love, passionlessness marches;
> in front of knowledge, love. (no. 67)

> To knowledge, wisdom is added;
> prudence gives birth to passionlessness. (no. 68)

Most of Evagrius's major works appear in the chapter, or century, form, that is, as collections of often-enigmatic aphorisms organized in groups of hundreds. His most important work is the great trilogy sometimes called the *Monachikos*, which mirrors the basic structure of his view of the mystical life. This consists of the *Praktikos*, one hundred chapters on the ascetic life, together with the *Gnostikos*, fifty chapters on how the "Gnostic," or true contemplative, teaches spiritual knowledge. The longest part of the trilogy is the great *Kephalaia Gnostica* (KG), six centuries of ninety chapters each, which give the heart of Evagrius's speculative mysticism. In addition, there is the important work on prayer, *On Prayer* (*De Oratione*), and a number of primarily ascetical works for monastics, such as the *Antirrhetikos* (a treatise on the eight principal sinful tendencies) and the *Mirror for Monks* and *The Mirror for Nuns*. Among the surviving letters, his *Letter to Melania* and the *Letter of Faith* are important for understanding his mystical thought. When carefully studied, Evagrius's chapters reveal a subtle and at times deliberately ambiguous mode of thought. His gnomic sayings are like the tips of mystical icebergs, revealing their true size and configuration only after prolonged meditation and extensive exploration beneath the surface.

ORIGENISM IN EVAGRIUS

The Two Creations

The Pontic master's basic view of reality, like Origen's, is realized in three stages — creation, fall and second creation, and the eventual return. The presence of movement, inequality, and evil in the world of our experience makes it necessary to postulate a first creation, a prior harmonious world of equal spiritual beings ("rationals" in Evagrius's terminology), as well as a future return of all spiritual beings to God and the eventual destruction of evil. The first creation, which enjoyed absolute unity with the Trinity, fell away from its contemplative perfection through "negligence." Evagrius is even less informative than was Origen about the essence of this primordial fault, one that lies deeper than the "sins" that take place in the second creation.

"If you are a theologian you truly pray. If you truly pray, you are a theologian."

— Evagrius Ponticus, *On Prayer*

The negligence of the first creation brought about God's immediate judgment on the "rationals" (i.e., creatures with intellects), and the production of the second creation, which is characterized by movement, multiplicity, and matter. This second creation is effected in and through Christ, the only unfallen rational. As the spiritual created being who is perfectly united to the Logos, the second person of the Trinity, he alone knows the essential principle of each thing that belongs to the second creation. The rationals are assigned conditions in the second creation in proportion to the degree of their negligence, winding up as angels, humans, or demons. The mind, or rational identity (*nous*), of each spiritual being descends or thickens into soul (*psyche*). The soul is composed of three elements: the rational element, sensuality, and irascibility. The rational predominates in angels, sensuality in humans, and irascibility in demons. God has given all three kinds of beings bodies adapted to their spiritual constitutions. These bodies indicate the state of *nous* within the creature and are also aids in the process of return to God. Humans, then, in the fallen second creation are composed of body and a soul with three parts: mind (*nous*), the sensual part, and the irascible part. According to God's providence, angels, humans, and demons will return eventually to their original unity, where body, soul and mind will become one entity again. The position that all creation will return — even the demons — was one of the teachings singled out for later attacks on both Origen and Evagrius.

Return

The return of the fallen rational creation to its source is accomplished in three stages. Evagrius says: "Christianity is the dogma of Christ our Savior. It is composed of ascetic living, of the contemplation of the physical world, and of the contemplation of God" (*Praktikos* no. 1). The two contemplative stages are subdivisions of the Gnostic life — the life of awareness. This threefold pattern was one of the Pontic abba's major innovations, an important prototype of the later distinction between the ascetical and the mystical, or the active life and the contemplative life. The three stages mark the levels by which *nous* is restored to its former place. As Evagrius summarizes: "The goal of ascetic living is to purify the intellect and to render it passionless; that of the contemplation of the physical world is to reveal the truth hidden in all beings; but to remove the intellect from all material things and to turn it toward the First Cause is a gift of the contemplation of God" (*Gnostikos* no. 49).

THE ASCETIC LIFE

In many ways Evagrius's most significant contribution is to be found in his exposition of ascetical theory. In this regard he fashioned tools of permanent value for later Christian spirituality. His major work on this theme is the *Praktikos*, which outlines the struggle of the monastic Christian to get rid of the evil aspects of the human condition and replace them with virtues. Evagrius developed a teaching on the eight evil or passionate thoughts or tendencies present in the soul through the pull of desire and irascibility and the deceptions of the fallen intellect. Each vice is encouraged by the demons who specialize in that form of temptation. Evagrius lists these forerunners of the Seven Deadly Sins as gluttony, impurity, avarice, depression, anger, impatient discouragement or dissatisfaction, vainglory, and pride. These tendencies make true contemplation impossible. The demons use them to keep the soul from becoming its true self. Evagrius's subtle and sensible exposition of the nature of these evil thoughts and the ways to recognize and combat them makes him one of the masters of what came to be called the "discernment of spirits."

In the *Praktikos* Evagrius demonstrates his nuanced understanding of the human condition in his exposition of the eight kinds of evil thoughts, how to recognize them and how to deal with them. Here from John Eudes Bamberger in *The Praktikos: Chapters on Prayer* is a sampling of his advice about anger. The abba clearly recognizes the great danger of anger:

> The most fierce passion is anger. In fact it is defined as a boiling and stirring up of wrath against one who has given injury — or is thought to have done so. It constantly irritates the soul and above all at the time of prayer it seizes the mind and flashes the picture of the offensive person before one's eyes. Then there comes a time when it persists longer, is transformed into indignation, stirs up alarming experiences by night. This is succeeded by a general debility of the body, malnutrition with its attendant pallor, and the illusion of being attacked by poisonous wild beasts. These four last mentioned consequences following upon indignation may be found to accompany many thoughts. (no. 11)

He also gives practical advice for combating anger:

> Reading, vigils and prayer — these are the things that lend stability to the wandering mind. Hunger, toil and solitude are the means of extinguishing the flames of desire. Turbid anger is calmed by the singing of Psalms, by patience and almsgiving. But all these practices are to be engaged in according to due measure and at the

appropriate times. What is untimely done, or done without measure, endures but a short time. And what is
short-lived is more harmful than profitable. (no. 15)

Let not the sun go down upon our anger lest by night
the demons come upon us to strike fear in our souls and
render our spirits more cowardly for the fight on the
morrow. For images of a frightful kind usually arise from
anger's disturbing influence. Indeed, there is nothing
more disposed to render the spirit inclined to desertion
than troubled irascibility. (no. 21)

Evagrius also recognizes that there is a useful form of anger:

Anger is given to us so that we might fight against the
demons and strive against every pleasure. Now it happens that the angels suggest spiritual pleasure to us and
the beatitude that is consequent upon it so as to encour-
age us to turn our anger against the demons. But these,
for their part, draw our anger to worldly desires and con-
strain us — contrary to our nature — to fight against our
fellow men to the end that, blinded in mind and falling
away from knowledge, our spirit should become a traitor
to virtue. (no. 24)

Evagrius emphasizes that the exterior asceticism of depri-
vation of sleep, food, and sex is a necessary but not sufficient
condition for undertaking the real struggle to control the
downward pull of vices such as anger. The goal of such ascetical struggle is to effect a transformation in the soul — to
achieve passionlessness, a necessary condition before moving
on to the two stages of contemplation. Evagrius's notion of

apatheia is not Stoic indifference or absence of feeling, but is rather "the health of the soul" (*Prak.* no. 56) that is attained through inner integration, what Evagrius's follower John Cassian translated as "purity of heart." In his *On Prayer* Evagrius says, "The state of prayer can be aptly described as a habitual state of imperturbable calm. It snatches to the heights of intelligible reality the spirit which loves wisdom and which is truly spiritualized by the most intense love" (no. 52). The passionless one, no longer under the influence of the vices and their attendant demons, is the person who is ready to engage in pure prayer.

THE CONTEMPLATIVE LIFE

> Knowledge! The great possession of man. It is a fellow-worker with prayer, acting to awaken the power of thought to contemplate the divine knowledge. (*On Prayer* no. 86)

Having overcome the pull of evil thoughts, the monk can proceed into the life of contemplation: first to the understanding of created reality, including a deeper understanding of the scriptures; and ultimately to the knowledge that *is* the Holy Trinity. However, the abba's wisdom is seen in the many ways by which he shows the interdependence of the monk's practical and contemplative lives. Perfect "health of the soul" comes about "when the spirit begins to see its own light, when it remains in a state of tranquility in the presence of the images it has during sleep and when it maintains its calm as it beholds the affairs of life" (*Prak.* no. 64). In the Preface to the *Praktikos* he describes the process succinctly:

The fear of God strengthens faith, my son, and conti-
nence in turn strengthens this fear. Patience and hope
make this latter virtue solid beyond all shaking and they
also give birth to *apatheia*. Now this *apatheia* has a child
called *agape*, who keeps the door to deep knowledge of
the created universe. Finally, to this knowledge succeed
theology and supreme beatitude. (*Prak.* Pref.).

This passionlessness, besides bearing love as its child, is
also the precondition for pure prayer for Evagrius. It is the
glory and light of the soul that make it possible for mind
to attain its own proper glory and light, that is, knowledge
(*gnosis*). The "contemplation of things" as mirrors of God is
divided into two major parts: the contemplation of corporeal
and of incorporeal beings. But Evagrius does not linger over
this stage; he is anxious to move on to the consideration of
the higher stage, where mind attains "essential knowledge of
the Holy Trinity."

Multiplicity and movement, the marks of created being,
characterize all knowledge below that of the Trinity. The
essential knowledge of the Trinity is realized by mind (*nous*)
when it has been restored to absolute simplicity: "Naked mind
is that which through the contemplation which concerns it
is united to the science of the Trinity" (*KG* 3.8). Every other
form of contemplation has some kind of determined object at
its base; contemplation of the Trinity is unlimited (*KG* 4.87–
88). This is the goal of Evagrius's teaching. The mind that
has attained this level can even be spoken of as divine, at
least by participation, or what the monk from Pontus would
call "reception" (*KG* 4.51; 5.81).

As Origen before him, Evagrius teaches that the process of return can take place only through the taking on of flesh by the preexistent Christ. The human mind (*nous*) ascends through the power of the Incarnate Christ: "Christ is the only one who has the Unity within him and he has received the judgment of the rationals" (*KG* 3.2). His descent makes possible our ascent and eventual divinization. In his *Letter to Melania* Evagrius presents the way in which naked mind attains a relationship with each of the divine persons of the Trinity. Just as in the natural order the body reveals the soul, which in turn reveals the mind, so mind itself functions as a "body" for the Spirit and the Word, who are the "soul" through which the Father works in mind (no. 4). This is the core of the abba's understanding of the mind's character as *imago Dei,* or as image of the perfect Image, that is, the Word (see *KG* 6.34). Citing Colossians 3:10, he says that the full renewal of the image will come when body, soul, and mind will cease to be separate:

> Just as the nature of human mind [*nous*] will be united to the Father, as it is his body, so too the names "soul" and "body" will be absorbed in the persons of the Son and Spirit, and will remain continually one nature and three persons of God and his image, as it was before the Incarnation and as it will be again, also after the Incarnation, because of the unanimity of wills. (*Letter to Melania* no. 5)

Evagrius never uses the term "mystical union," and even the standard Greek terms for union are absent from his vocabulary. But it is clear that the essential knowledge involves a "merging" with the Trinity that he sometimes speaks

of in daring fashion. The *Letter to Melania* compares the fall
of the rationals from archetypal union with God and their
return to it in terms of the image of an "intelligible sea":

> When minds flow back to him like torrents into the sea,
> he changes them all completely into his own nature,
> color, and taste. They will no longer be many but one
> in his unending and inseparable unity, because they are
> united and joined with him. And as in the fusion of
> rivers with the sea no addition in its nature or varia-
> tion in its color or taste is to be found, so also in the
> fusion of minds with the Father no duality of natures or
> quaternity of persons comes about. (no. 6)

Before the fall, the rationals "were at one with him without distinction." Sin, like the earth that separates the rivers
from the sea, divided the rationals from the Father. But the
end will be like the beginning, so that "he who observes the
making perfect of all intellects is amazed greatly and marvels
because he sees all these various distinct knowledges as they
merge into one essential and unique knowledge, and that all
those become this one, forever" (*Letter to Melania* no. 12). In
this same letter, however, the abba distinguishes between the
created nature of the rationals and their eternal existence in
the divine mind. The rationals are always described as being
merely "receptive" of the Trinity, not identical with it. Still,
his affirmation of eventual reunification of the rationals with
God suggests a final indistinct union in which the spiritual
creation becomes one with its source.

Evagrius's teaching on the ascent of mind through the
power of the incarnate Christ centers on three closely related
activities: understanding created reality (*theoria*); essential

knowledge (*gnosis*), that is, the knowledge that *is* the Holy Trinity; and prayer. Sometimes the terms for these activities are used interchangeably — for instance, prayer is used both for all the activities by which mind ascends and for the unitive knowing that is the goal. While some levels of prayer can be considered preludes to the highest essential knowledge (*On Prayer* no. 86), prayer in the truest sense is coextensive with essential knowledge of the Trinity, as we learn from the famous axiom: "If you are a theologian you truly pray. If you truly pray, you are a theologian" (*On Prayer* no. 60). What the abba calls "pure prayer" or "true prayer" is the gradual stripping away of all images and forms in order to attain formless and conceptless direct contact with the unnumbered and formless Trinity. "Prayer is the continual intercourse of the spirit with God. What state of soul then is required that the spirit might thus strain after its Master without wavering, living constantly with him without intermediary?" (*On Prayer* no. 3).

> For everyone, even those who do not feel called to take up the monastic or ascetic life, the sound practical advice Evagrius presents on developing a life of virtue and of prayer is timeless.

Many commentators have noted that Evagrius's equation of pure prayer with essential knowledge of the Trinity is one of the most distinctive contributions of his thought, especially within the context of monastic life. He is one of the first who made contemplative prayer the essence of the monastic life and thus linked the forces of monasticism and mysticism in a powerful way. The affirmation that such prayer attains unmediated contact with God shows that while the desert abba did not use the notion of divine presence as an explicit category of his mystical theory, this central thread of Christian mysticism is implied in his writings.

Close study of Evagrius's writings reveals one of the tensions present in the monastic layer of Christian mysticism throughout its history: the uneasy coexistence between the universality of the message of the return to God held out to all on one hand, and on the other the apparent conviction that the contemplative goal of pure prayer that gains access to essential knowledge of the Trinity is accessible only to advanced monastics who have undergone years of ascetical and theoretical training. As he puts it in one place, "By true prayer a monk becomes another angel, for he ardently longs to see the face of the father in heaven" (*On Prayer* no. 113).

For Evagrius the monk who has become like the angels does not lose all connection with and responsibility for his fellow humans or for the rest of God's creation. At the conclusion of a series of beatitudes on pure prayer and the monastic life (*On Prayer* nos. 117–23), he declares, "A monk is one who is separated from all and united with all" (*On Prayer* no. 124). The ritual of dissociation that formed monastic withdrawal did separate the monk from the wider community, but its goal was to bring the monastic into the divine harmony of the original creation. The achievement of this union gave the monk a new perspective and communion with all humans, as well as a new and powerful role in Christianity.

This text suggests why the monastic movement was institutionally and spiritually so essential to Christian mysticism in the centuries to come, and also why Evagrius's synthesis of the mystical and the monastic elements in early Christianity was so important.

CONCLUSION

Even today, Abba Evagrius has a word of salvation for those who seek out his wisdom. His life itself speaks eloquently to those who would serve as counselors or spiritual guides — that it is when we learn humility and silence that we find the truth of things, and only then are we fit to offer advice to others. For scholars and writers on the inner life he offers the example of one who made study and writing a spiritual discipline, oriented to the good of the community. As with so many of the mystics, he inspires us by the intensity of his search for the presence of God.

For everyone, even those who do not feel called to take up the monastic or ascetic life, the sound practical advice Evagrius presents on developing a life of virtue and of prayer is timeless. Meditation on his proverbs richly repays the seeker. As he says:

> The Holy Spirit takes compassion on our weakness, and though we are impure he often comes to visit us. If he should find our spirit praying to him out of love for the truth he then descends upon it and dispels the whole army of thoughts and reasonings that beset it. And too he urges it on to the works of spiritual prayer. (*On Prayer* no. 62)

SUGGESTIONS FOR FURTHER READING

Many of Evagrius's writings are not available in English. Among those that are, see Evagrius Ponticus, *Praktikos: Chapters on Prayer*, translated by John Eudes Bamberger (Kalamazoo, Mich.: Cistercian Publications, 1970); and *The Mind's Long Journey to the Holy Trinity: The "Ad Monachos" of Evagrius Ponticus*, translated by Jeremy Driscoll (Collegeville, Minn.: Liturgical Press, 1993). For the context of Evagrius, see Andrew Louth, *The Origins of the Christian Mystical Tradition: From Plato to Denys* (Oxford: Clarendon Press, 1981), chapter 6; and Douglas Burton-Christie, *The Word in the Desert: Scripture and the Quest for Holiness in Early Christian Monasticism* (New York: Oxford University Press, 1993).

Three

Prayer and Purity of Heart

JOHN CASSIAN

LIFE

We don't know where or when Cassian was born. Even his name is not completely certain. Though others referred to him in documents as "Cassianus," the only name he uses in his own writings is "Ioannes," that is, John. His birth date has been narrowed to the 360s and his death to a few years after 430, situating him as an almost exact contemporary of Augustine. He was a native Latin speaker, though fluent in Greek, and it is this bilingualism coupled with his enthusiasm for the monasticism of the East that helped him make his contribution to the development of mysticism. It was John Cassian who brought the teachings and the practices of Eastern monasticism to the Latin West; he thus stands as a major founding figure of Latin mysticism. As a young man he and his friend Germanus traveled to Palestine and entered a monastery in Bethlehem. After a few years, inspired by contact with a famous Egyptian abba named Pinufius, Cassian and Germanus obtained permission to visit the monasteries in Egypt. Their travels in Lower Egypt, interviewing the famous abbas of the desert, lasted at least fifteen years. These experiences profoundly and permanently shaped Cassian's understanding of monasticism, an understanding that he later strove to convey to his monks in Gaul.

Cassian was a convinced Origenist who was deeply influenced by the teachings of Evagrius Ponticus, though due to the fierce Origenist controversy neither Origen nor Evagrius ever appear by name in Cassian's writings. Because of the controversy and the persecution that devastated Egyptian monasticism, Cassian and Germanus fled Egypt around 400. We know that they went first to John Chrysostom at Constantinople. Later when Chrysostom himself came under attack, Cassian went on to Rome, where he spent some years. He settled finally in Marseilles in southern Gaul around 415 and established two monasteries (one might have been for women, headed by his sister). Here he undertook the tasks of composing his accounts of Eastern monasticism and advising the Gallic bishops about how monks should live and how they should pursue spiritual perfection. Somewhere in these moves Germanus must have died, but Cassian is silent on this deeply personal event as on so many others.

TRANSMITTING
EASTERN MONASTICISM

Cassian's major works were the *Conferences* (*Conlationes*) (ca. 426–29) and the *Institutes of the Coenobites* (*Institutiones*) (ca. 430). Each of the conferences is cast as a conversation in which he and Germanus are taught about the interior life of anchorites (hermits) and cenobites (monks in community) by one of the great abbas of the desert. In the *Institutes* he describes the external practices of monks living in community. For Cassian, no form of monastic living elsewhere could match the excellence of Egyptian monasticism, and he was determined to bring this wisdom of the desert to the West. His writings were the most important links between Eastern and Western monasticism for over a millennium. The other founders of Western mysticism, Ambrose and Augustine, were devotees of the monastic ideal; Cassian was completely monastic. His total life experience had been a monastic one, and his major writings were directed only to monks. As important leaders of dioceses, both Ambrose and Augustine had obligations to the world of lay Christians, and they played their part in the birth of a distinctive lay spirituality. Cassian had few ties to that world; for him Christian perfection was reserved only for monastics.

Indeed, for Cassian the church was meant to be a monastic institution. He is the earliest witness (*Conf.* 18.5) to the oft-repeated monastic claim that the first Christians in Jerusalem were actually a cenobitic monastic community and that it was the laxity of later ages that allowed for the split between the true monastic Christians and their second-rate lay counterparts. In a sense it is true to say that Cassian thought of monasticism not as an element in a Christian society but as the Christian alternative to society. Much more than Ambrose or Augustine, this transplanted ascetic stands at the beginning of a two-tiered model of Christian spirituality in which higher, mystical perfection is believed open only to the monastics who have fled the world and who live lives of perfect chastity.

Cassian was an important conduit by which the teaching of Origen and Evagrius came to the West. He wrote primarily in a practical vein to instruct Western monks in the values and practices of his heroes of the desert. This practical side is seen in his frequent emphasis on the necessity of testing spiritual teaching against experience. While his writing is not meant to be systematic, the Evagrian system lurks behind it. Conference 14, given by the Abba Nestorius, deals with spiritual knowledge, dividing it into two parts: "First there is practical, that is, active knowledge, which is perfected in correcting moral actions and purging vices; and second, the theoretical knowledge, which consists in the contemplation of divine things and the grasp of the most sacred meanings [of scripture]" (*Conf.* 14.1).

Active knowledge has two basic operations. The first is the negative task of coming to understand and root out the eight principal vices or evil inclinations that Cassian adopted from Evagrius and introduced to the West — gluttony, lust, and avarice (affecting the desiring power of the soul); anger, sadness, and discouragement (attacking the irascible part of the soul — its power of rejection); and finally vainglory and pride (vices peculiar to the soul's reasoning power). Cassian's anthropology is a simplified version of Evagrius, though in keeping with Western interests, he puts stress on monastic perfection as producing the restoration of the soul's likeness to God, especially as we pass from the negative to the positive side of practical knowledge.

The positive pole of this practical knowledge is less easily schematized, though Cassian emphasizes humility and discretion as the primary guiding forces in virtuous action. His moral theology is best approached not by attempting to grasp how he views each individual monastic virtue, but by recognizing that it is the acquisition of purity of heart (*puritas cordis*) and love (*caritas*) that gives meaning to all moral effort.

In the first conference Abba Moses, whom Cassian considered the "Chief of all the saints" (*Institutes* 10.25), despite his earlier criminal past, sets out the guiding map of the monastic journey by distinguishing between the ultimate end of the monastic life, which is identified as the kingdom of God, and the direction or aim that enables us to reach the goal. "The end of our profession, as we have said, is the kingdom of God or kingdom of heaven, but its direction . . . is purity of heart, without which it is impossible for anyone to reach that end" (*Conf.* 1.4). This vocabulary is taken over from Evagrius, but it abandons the desert monk's favorite term, *apatheia* (passionlessness), for the more positive and scriptural connotation of *puritas cordis* (purity of heart, Matt. 5:8: "Blessed are the pure of heart, for they shall see God").

The underlying doctrine is not really different. Evagrius's *apatheia*, as we have seen, was far from Stoic forms of indifference. It was essentially a state of tranquility or detachment ("the health of the soul" [*Praktikos* no. 56]) achieved through overcoming the eight evil tendencies. Evagrius claimed that passionlessness gave birth to love (*Praktikos* pref.); Cassian brings the two even closer together. While he can describe purity of heart negatively as the avoidance of vices, positively speaking, purity of heart is nothing else but love (*Conf.* 1.7). The relation between the two is perhaps best expressed in *Institutes* 4.43: "Purity of heart is acquired by the flowering of the virtues, and the perfection of apostolic charity is possessed by means of purity of heart."

Matthew 5:8 had promised the vision of God to those who were pure of heart. Hence it was an easy step for Cassian to understand the purity of heart that leads to the kingdom of God in terms of preparation for contemplation. In Conference 10.10 he describes the purifying activity of his famous formula of unceasing prayer (Ps. 69:2) as leading to "invisible and celestial contemplations and to that inexpressible fire of prayer experienced by very few." We may take it that charity, contemplation, and union are all correlative terms expressing different but interrelated aspects of the second or theoretical stage of spiritual knowledge.

"The entire goal of the monk and the perfection of the heart moves toward continual and uninterrupted perseverance in prayer."

—John Cassian, Conference 9

When Cassian turns to the discussion of theoretical knowledge in Conference 14, he departs from the model of Evagrius. Rather than outlining the two types of contemplation (knowledge of created things and knowledge of the divine) favored by the abba, he instead follows Origen in discussing theoretical knowledge or contemplation in terms of the proper mode of understanding scripture. "Theoretical knowledge is divided into two parts, that is, into historical interpretation and spiritual understanding. . . . There are three types of spiritual knowledge: tropology, allegory, anagogy" (*Conf.* 14.8). Cassian goes on to illustrate the famous four senses of scripture in a classic text based on Paul's reading of Abraham's two wives in Galatians 4:22–23. History is the past historical fact of Abraham having two sons from two different women; allegory is the way in which the two women prefigure the two covenants of the Old and New Testaments. "Anagogy climbs up from spiritual mysteries to higher and more sacred celestial secrets," that is, the message that the Jerusalem on high is our true mother (see Gal. 4:26–27). Finally, tropology is the moral explanation according to which the two covenants are the practical and theoretical knowledge that instruct the Jerusalem of the soul. Cassian (following Origen) ties his higher knowledge more directly to the biblical text than Evagrius did. He makes constant reference to biblical passages understood in a highly spiritual way, and he insists that the proper grasp of the Bible is dependent on moral effort rather than mere study: purity of heart rather than knowledge of the commentators is the key (see *Instit.* 5.34). Conference 14.10 uses an image in which constant meditation on the scripture eventually forms the Ark of the Covenant within the soul, that is, the meaning of the Bible becomes connatural.

Cassian makes use of another general pattern, also based on Evagrius and Origen, to structure his account of the monk's progress to perfection. Conference 3 of Abba Paphnutius centers on three renunciations:

The first is that by which we despise all the riches and resources of the world with our bodies. The second that by which we reject former activities, vices and desires of the soul and the flesh; the third that by which we recall our minds from every present visible thing in order to contemplate only what lies ahead and to desire the things that are invisible. (*Conf.* 3.6)

These three renunciations, which may be compared with the three motivations for good actions considered in Conference 11 (fear of hell, hope of heaven, and love of virtue), portray a broad program of ascent in which the first two comprise the level of active knowledge, while the third embraces theoretical knowledge. They are also compared to the three books of Solomon: Proverbs teaches the renunciation of the flesh and earthly things; Ecclesiastes counsels the vanity of all creation; and the Song of Songs presents the third renunciation "in which the mind transcending everything visible is joined to God's Word by the contemplation of heavenly things" (*Conf.* 3.6). This threefold Origenist theme, which correlates the Song of Songs with the highest form of spiritual knowledge, was dear to Ambrose, but Cassian differs from the bishop and from Jerome in making little use of the erotic language of the Song as an instrument for mystical expression.

One final theological note can be added here. Cassian became the spokesman for those monks who were upset by Augustine's late predestinarian teaching on grace that seemed to deny human freedom and therefore the moral effort of asceticism. Cassian takes up this issue in Conference 13. He represents the protest of an older, more synergistic view of the relation of grace and human action in the face of the rending quarrels that erupted over the teaching of Pelagius. Cassian is no Pelagian, however; he insists on the necessity of grace for the attainment of purity of heart and perfect charity. Yet from the Augustinian perspective he seems to want to have it both ways. Though some texts insist that "the beginning of good will in us is granted by God's inspiration" (*Conf.* 3.19), other passages make it clear that Cassian thought that at least in some cases grace was given to those "who labor and sweat for it" (*Instit.* 12.14).

PURE AND UNCEASING PRAYER

For Cassian pure and unceasing prayer was the essence of the monastic life. "The entire goal of the monk and the perfection of the heart moves toward continual and uninterrupted perseverance in prayer," as Isaac says at the beginning of Conference 9. The goal thus announced he expands on in Conference 10.6–7 in one of his more important mystical passages. Since in prayer we see Jesus according to the level of purification we have attained, we behold him either in his humble and fleshly state, "or, with the internal gaze of the mind, as glorified and coming in the glory of his majesty" (*Conf.* 10.6). In order to reach such a vision, whose scriptural warrant is found in the account of the Transfiguration (Matt. 17:1–8), we must withdraw into solitude so that while still dwelling in the body we come to share some likeness of the future state when God will be all in all (1 Cor. 15:18). Thus, the goal of prayer is to be absorbed into the loving union that binds the persons of the Trinity, as Cassian says in a passage reminiscent of a text from Origen's *On First Principles:*

Then will be perfectly fulfilled in us our Savior's prayer
when he prayed to his Father for his disciples, "So that
the love with which you have loved me may be in them
and they in us" (John 17:26), and again, "That they all
may be one as you, Father in me and I in you, and that
they may be one in us" (John 17:21). The perfect love
with which "he first loved us" (1 John 4:10) will pass
into our heart's affection, . . . and that unity which now
belongs to the Father and the Son will be transfused
into our mind and understanding. (*Conf.* 10.7)

This unity, in which whatever we breathe or think or speak
about *is* God, is an image or a pledge of the heavenly state
to come. It is the "one unending prayer" that is the goal of
the monastic life. Deeply Evagrian as Cassian's view is, the
numerous Johannine references give his unceasing prayer a
more christological character than what we find in Evagrius's
presentation.

To understand his teaching about how it is possible for the
monk to pray always, Cassian's Conferences 9 and 10 must
be taken together. Both deal with the preparation for perfect
prayer, and especially with the method by which it is to be
attained. In the more extensive treatment in Conference 9,
the preparation involves not only overcoming vices but also
liberation from distractions and from all earthly concerns. Cassian here provides a small treatise on prayer in general and
on four types of prayer in particular: supplications, petitions,
intercessions, and thanksgiving. After this, to illustrate the
"higher and more excellent state formed by the contemplation
of God and the ardor of charity" (9.18), he turns from these
four types to a commentary on the Lord's Prayer (9.18–24).

In the tenth conference, however, Cassian encourages another form of prayer in order to achieve the goal of cease-less prayer: the constant repetition of a single short verse, in this case the form known as the "Deus in adjutorium" taken from Psalm 69:2 ("O God, come to my aid; Lord, make haste to help me") (10.10–11). Both the Our Father and the "Deus in adjutorium" are described as formulas, that is, as scriptural forms of meditation that serve as essential food for the soul in its progress toward the highest stages of prayer. While Cassian stresses the advantages of the latter formula because it concentrates the attention and expresses the pov-erty of the human situation, his position seems to be that a variety of modes, methods, and formulas are allowed, but the ones rooted in scripture are preferable.

In both conferences this study of method brings Cas-sian back to a new and deeper consideration of the goal of prayer. These passages are among the most important for understanding his mysticism (*Conf.* 9.25–27; 10.11). The controlling image in these texts is fire; the key themes are passivity, rapture, ineffability, and transiency. While earlier passages in Conference 9 had mentioned "very fervent and fiery prayers" in connection with thanksgiving (9.15), the level of prayer that Cassian speaks of in 9.25 indicates a higher state of the ineffable "prayer of fire known and expe-rienced by so few." This prayer, as the discussions in 9.26–27 and 10.11 indicate, is always a divine gift, one given in a variety of ways that show that Cassian's doctrine of the higher stages of prayer is still a fluid one. Most often, it has its source in compunction, but it finds its expression in "unspeakable joy" and "inexpressible groans" (9.27). It can-not be communicated in words, because it takes place when

the combined knowing powers of the soul pass beyond themselves (inwardly or outwardly) in a rapture of the mind (9.31;
10.10) or a rapture of the heart (10.11). The examples given
indicate that it is of brief duration, though Cassian does not
attempt to describe this aspect in more detail. Such prayer,
he says, follows the model given by Jesus (citing Luke 5:16
and 22:44). Antony of the desert is brought in as well, especially his statement "that prayer is not perfect in which the
monk is conscious of himself or the fact that he is praying"
(*Conf.* 9.31).

The parallel passage in Conference 10.11 brings out another
dimension of this form of prayer. Here Cassian speaks of praying the Psalms in such a way that they conform perfectly to
our own experience. "Receiving the same movement of the
heart in which the Psalm was first sung or written, we become,
as it were, its author, anticipating the meaning rather than
following it." This way of reading or praying the scripture
from within is characteristic of the exegetical nature of early
Christian mysticism, particularly as we have seen it realized in
Origen. Here Cassian says that it prepares for the passage to
that kind of pure prayer treated in the previous conference,
which he now summarizes:

> [This prayer] is not concerned with any consideration
> of an image, nor characterized by any sound nor set
> of words. It comes forth from a fiery mental intention
> through an ineffable rapture of the heart by means of an
> inexplicable burst of the spirit. Freed from all sensations
> and visible concerns, the mind pours itself out to God
> with unspeakable groans and sighs (Rom. 8:26). (*Conf.*
> 10.11)

One other conference sheds further light on Cassian's understanding of mystical prayer and contemplation. In Conference 19 Abba John discusses the relationship between the lives of hermits and monks. He argues that the heights of contemplation can be reached only through the solitary life in the desert, but because of the dangers of this existence for those who have not yet reached perfect purity of heart, it is safer to pursue one's salvation in the supportive context of the community. Cassian claims that only a very few abbas have been able to combine both types of life (19.9). This extended treatment of the goals and advantages of the two forms of monastic life allows for considerable attention to the ecstatic prayer that is the identifying mark of the hermit, but (as we see on the basis of 9.25–27) need not be totally absent from the life of the monk in community. Abba John admits that while in the desert he was so *frequently* caught up in such raptures that he forgot he was still in the body (19.4), but he allows that as more hermits began to people the wilderness, "the fire of divine contemplation began to grow cold," so that he decided to retreat to the monastery where "what I lose of the heights of contemplation I get back by the submission of obedience" (*Conf.* 19.5). John considers the ecstatic prayer he enjoyed in the desert as a means of being united with Christ. As 19.8 declares, the hermit's goal is "to have a mind emptied of all earthly things (as far as human weakness allows) and thus to be united to Christ."

It is clear from these conferences that Cassian, like Evagrius, believed that prayer was the essence of the life of perfection and that pure and unceasing prayer provided an immediate access to God's presence as a foretaste of heaven.

Though his understanding of what later ages would call mystical prayer is broad and somewhat diffuse, including a variety of experiences, Cassian is conscious of the need for some discriminations (*Conf.* 9.26–29). "*Theoria,* that is, the contemplation of God, is the one thing in relation to which all the merits of our righteousness and all our virtuous efforts are secondary" (*Conf.* 23.3). Contemplation, of course, implies the vision of God, at least in its higher stages, and mention of "the vision of God alone" (*Conf.* 9.17) appears fairly often in his discussions of prayer and contemplation. "Contemplation" itself is an elastic term for the monk. Although he specifies various kinds of contemplation in a number of places, his real interest is in contemplation conceived of as the progressive conformation of the soul to God.

ACTION, CONTEMPLATION, AND UNION

Cassian's understanding of the relation of contemplation to action appears mostly in his discussions of the respective advantages of the two forms of monasticism: the eremitical life of the hermit and the cenobitical life of monks in community. It is not hard to find passages that express the theoretical supremacy of the eremitical life of contemplation with its goal of ecstatic experience. But in reality things are not that simple. Conference 9.25–27 shows that rapture can be found in the cenobitical life, and in Conference 19 Cassian shows that he realizes that both the solitary and the community forms of monasticism mix action and contemplation, though in differing ways. Cassian did not work out a clear and coherent solution to the relationship of contemplative absorption in God and active love for the monastic brethren (e.g., *Conf.* 24–26), and the issue continued to trouble medieval mystics, especially monastic ones. Perhaps we may take as his basic position something he said about the relation of physical labor to contemplative prayer: "There is a mutual and inseparable link between the two" (*Conf.* 9.2).

> *Contemporary Christians, lay and monastic alike, find deep wisdom in his insistence that charity and hospitality should prevail over all else, even personal solitude and contemplation.*

For Cassian, contemplation, or the vision of God in a perfected soul, is also described as a joining or uniting of the soul to God in loving union. Cassian had a definite if not developed doctrine of union with God, even though his writings do not express what later mystics would characterize as an immediate consciousness of God's presence (*Conf.* 10.7). The transplanted Easterner's main concern was with conveying to his Latin audience knowledge of the ascetical practices of Egypt, but he does more than leave his readers at the entrance to contemplation. Especially in Conferences 9 and 10 he conveys to them something of the inexpressible mystery of more direct contact with God. At the end of Conference 8, Abba Serenus provides a wonderful nautical image for this mystery:

Our brief and simple words have drawn the ship of this Conference to the safe harbor of silence from the deep sea of questions, in which deep indeed, as the breath of the Divine Spirit drives us deeper in, is ever opened up a wider and boundless space reaching beyond the sight of the eye. (8.25)

By the time of Cassian's death, Latin monasticism was developing on its own. With regard to the history of mysticism, it was the new institution of monasticism that would be the main social force for nurturing mystical texts and practices and for transmitting them to future generations.

CONCLUSION

The enthusiasm of Cassian for purity of heart and pure prayer communicates its fire to us through the many intervening centuries. Moreover, we still have among us men and women monastics who are his spiritual descendants. Certainly contemporary Christians, lay and monastic alike, find deep wisdom in his insistence that charity and hospitality should prevail over all else, even personal solitude and contemplation. Those who struggle to focus and to pray in the severely fractured modern world are inspired and encouraged by Cassian's simple "Deus in adjutorium" (O God, come to my assistance; O Lord, make haste to help me), as a way to pray always.

SUGGESTED READING

There is now a fine and complete translation of the *Conferences*. See *John Cassian: The Conferences*, translated by Boniface Ramsey, Ancient Christian Writers 57 (New York: Paulist Press, 1997). An old translation of Cassian's *Institutes* can be found in vol. 11 of the Second Series of A *Select Library of Nicene and Post-Nicene Fathers*, edited by Philip Schaff and Henry Wace. A good introduction to Cassian is Columba Stewart, *Cassian the Monk* (New York: Oxford University Press, 1998). See also Philip Rousseau, *Ascetics, Authority, and the Church in the Age of Jerome and Cassian* (Oxford: Oxford University Press, 1978).

Four

Compunction

GREGORY THE GREAT

LIFE

The world Gregory grew up in was a terrible place. He was born around 540, and his boyhood saw the horrors of the Ostrogothic War that devastated Italy for twenty years. The bubonic plague ravaged the Mediterranean world in the 540s. Then, after some years of peace, the Lombard invasion began in 568. Civilization, as aristocratic Roman families like his had known it, was in ruins. Hoping to escape "from the ship-wreck of this life" to a "safe haven," Gregory entered the monastery. He devoted himself to rigorous asceticism, con-templative prayer, and biblical exegesis. But the retreat into contemplative peace did not last long. Gregory's talents were recognized early. In 579 Pope Pelagius II called upon him to serve the church as papal ambassador to the imperial court in Constantinople, where Gregory's diplomatic and administra-tive abilities proved to be outstanding. When the pope died of the plague in 590, an anguished Gregory was the unanimous choice to succeed him.

Gregory the Great's pontificate (590–604) occurred in the middle of the transition from the world of the late antique Christian Roman Empire to the Christendom of the Middle Ages. The massive disturbances of his time convinced Gre-gory of the imminence of the end of the world, but this very fact, as well as his typically Roman sense of responsibility and his personal fortitude, led him to efforts that would have daunted even the most vigorous (and Gregory suffered from ill health for the whole of his pontificate). His prodigious political and ecclesiastical activity belies the naïve conviction that mystics and contemplatives usually have little effect on the real world of power and politics. But for Gregory the active life entailed extreme personal sacrifice. Some years later, as pope, he reflected back on his time in the mon-astery and commented on the painful but necessary tension between action and contemplation, as he wrote to a friend:

My unhappy intellectual soul, pierced with the wound of its own distraction, remembers how it used to be in the monastery in those days, when all time's fleeting objects were beneath it because it rose high above everything temporal. It thought only about heavenly things, so that

while still held in the body it had already passed beyond
the prison of the flesh in contemplation. . . . But now the
beauty of that spiritual repose is over, and the contact
with worldly men and their affairs, which is a necessary
part of my duties as bishop, has left my soul defiled
with earthly activities. . . . Now I am tossed about on the
waves of a great sea and my soul, like a ship, is buffeted
by the winds of a powerful storm. (*Dialogues,* Book 1,
Praef.)

WRITINGS

In his theological and spiritual writings Gregory can be seen
as the first medieval spiritual author. Almost all of these
works were put in their final form in the 590s, during the early
years of his pontificate. Gregory, like the other great mystical
authors of the early church, was above all an exegete and
a preacher. His massive *Moralia on Job,* among the longest
patristic works, was finished possibly as early as 591. The
twenty-two *Homilies on Ezekiel* contain some of his most
profound mystical teachings. They were preached during
592–93, the years that the Lombards besieged Rome (Gregory had to buy them off with five hundred pounds of gold).
The *Forty Gospel Homilies* for the liturgical year were mostly
delivered during 591 and 592.

Gregory's works were addressed to rather different audiences. The *Moralia* were written as moral interpretations of
the book of Job, composed primarily for his fellow monks,
while the *Gospel Homilies* were preached to the whole Christian community. The *Homilies on Ezekiel* seem to have taken
an intermediate position, being preached to a select group

that included both monks and laity. His *Book of Pastoral Rule*, intended to provide bishops and priests with guidance for living, was immensely important for the Middle Ages. Perhaps even more influential were his *Dialogues*, in which he recounted the lives and miraculous deeds of the holy men of sixth-century Italy. Read and used for centuries, it contains our only source for the life of Benedict of Nursia, the father of Western monasticism.

The pope's position as a major intermediary in the transmission of early Western mysticism to the Christendom of the Middle Ages is nowhere better displayed than in his insistence that it is only in and through study of the Bible that contemplation is possible. In commenting on the mysterious four animals of Ezekiel's vision, Gregory compares their walking about (Ezek. 1:9) with the moral interpretation of scripture and their flying upward with contemplative reading:

> The animals are lifted up from the earth when the holy ones are suspended in contemplation. The more a saint progresses in understanding scripture, the more scripture progresses in him. . . . This is what happens — you sense that the words of sacred scripture are heavenly if you yourself, enkindled through the grace of contemplation, are lifted up to heavenly things. When the reader's intellectual soul is pierced by supernal love, the wonderful and ineffable power of the sacred text is truly acknowledged. (*Hom. on Ez.* 1.7.8)

Gregory's writings are known for their lugubrious tone, especially when the monk-pope dwells on the dangers of life in the world and the trials of the married state, but as his

Moralia on Job show, his major concern was with the practical application of belief in the great mysteries, especially of Christ and the church, for individual behavior. While all the patriarchs and saints of the Old Testament are prophetic types of Christ, the figure of Job the patient sufferer, whose troubles foretell those of Christ on the cross, was a favorite of Gregory's. For him Job was the complete Christ, not only the head but also the members of his body, the church. Gregory's emphasis on moral and spiritual interiority, that is, on plumbing beneath the surface to uncover the roots of right action, leads to the optimistic teaching that Christians, while still in this life, can attain a partial vision of God, the vision that is contemplation.

Despite bemoaning how terrible things are in this life from day to day, Gregory retains an underlying sense of the triumph of joy and peace, if not in this world, certainly in the one to come. To love and long for this goal in the midst of suffering is what we are called to as followers of Job-Christ. The power of longing desire is what transforms the suffering we undergo, and even the sins we continue to commit, into stages of growth on the way for those who never relinquish the urgent movement forward. Gregory is the theologian of suffering, but it is a suffering of patient acceptance, not voluntary, induced suffering. For the pope pain and struggle are the mark of the human condition: "Human life on earth is warfare" (Job 7:1). But for him the essential, unrelenting struggle is between the present world of false values and the true values of the world to come. Time after time the pope highlights this oscillation between the outer world of trouble and worldly concerns, and the inner world of spiritual repose and joy. This opposition forms the theological basis for one of his most important contributions to the later history of Western spirituality, his teaching on compunction.

COMPUNCTION

In Acts 2:37 those who heard Peter's speech at Pentecost were "pierced to the heart." This "piercing" is the meaning of compunction for Gregory, the "Doctor of Compunction," precisely because of his deeply felt sense of the radical insufficiency of all terrestrial goods in relation to those of the heavenly world. Thus, his notion of compunction is not restricted to sorrow for sin (though this is vital); it involves the whole of the Christian's attitude toward present existence in relation to the underlying desire for the stability and joy of heaven. Central to his thought is the distinction between two kinds of compunction:

> There are two main kinds of compunction, because the soul thirsting for God is first pierced with fear and later with love. She first is overcome with weeping because she remembers her sins and fears eternal punishment for them. Then, when fear abates through prolonged sorrow and worry, a kind of security is already born from the confidence of pardon and the intellectual soul is inflamed with a love for heavenly joys. Thus the perfect compunction of fear draws the intellectual soul to the compunction of love. (*Dial.* 3.34.2)

For Gregory, compunction is not just sorrow for sin, as it sometimes came to be interpreted in later Western sources, but it is a total commitment to the whole Christian life, one that begins with sorrow for sin but that finds its real power in the compunction of love. Gregory reveals his own deep experiences of compunction in the reading of scripture:

> Through the grace of the Lord Almighty it often happens that certain things in scripture are better understood when God's word is read in private. The soul, conscious of its faults when it recognizes what it hears, pierces itself with the dart of pain and transfixes itself with the sword of compunction so that it can do nothing but weep and wash away its stains in floods of tears. In the midst of this, the soul is at times taken up to contemplate sublime things, the desire for which tortures it with a sweet weeping. (*Hom. on Ez.* 2.2.1)

Gregory's distinction between the compunction of fear and the compunction of love is brought out more clearly in his exposition of the four motives of the soul for compunction: first, when it remembers its own evils and *where it was,* that is, in sin; second, when it fears God's judgments and *where it will be,* perhaps in hell; third, when it bewails the evils of the present life *where it is,* that is, in the world; and fourth, when it contemplates the good things of the heavenly home and mourns *where it is not,* that is, in heaven (*Moralia on Job* 23.21.41). The first two relate to the lower tears of fear, the latter two to the upper tears of love. As the pope develops this theme in *Moralia* 12, the compunction of love takes on the character of a contemplative experience. Another text explicitly draws compunction and contemplation together: "When the mind is lifted up to lofty things through the engine, as it were, of compunction, it contemplates everything about itself as beneath it, with a more certain judgment" (*Mor.* 1.34.48).

Compunction leads to contemplation, and both are meant to nourish our concern for our neighbor, especially in the case of the clergy. He advises bishops, "When we feel inner compunction we must also become zealous for the lives of those entrusted to our care. The bitterness of compunction should not affect us so as to turn us away from the concerns of our neighbor" (*Hom. on the Gospels* 17.11). Gregorian compunction, then, is a rich and unifying spiritual force involving sorrow for sin, religious awe before the divine judge, detachment from the world, intense longing for heaven, contemplative self-awareness, and even the sweet sorrow that accompanies the necessary descent from the heights of the immediate experience of God. To grasp it in its many dimensions is to be firmly grounded in Gregory's spiritual sensibility at its most vital. The close connection between compunction and contemplation also helps us understand this second major theme of Gregory's mysticism.

CONTEMPLATION

Though Gregory the Great wrote no treatise on contemplation, the theme is present throughout his works. To present his thinking more systematically than he did, we will arrange this account around five issues: (a) the nature of contemplation; (b) the role of contemplation in the history of salvation; (c) how contemplation becomes accessible to the believer through Christ; (d) preparation for contemplation; and finally (e) contemplation and action.

What is contemplation for Gregory? Contemplation in the proper sense may be broadly understood as "attentive regard for God alone." Though the primary sensory analogy invoked is that of vision or sight, "regard" also allows for a notion of "respectful listening" that helps us to do justice to the many auditory images that the pope employs for describing our most intimate relation to God. Humanity was created for contemplative vision; it is our one goal. It is also an impossible attainment, at least in any perfect sense, given the incomprehensibility of God. Gregory's sense of the over-whelming divine majesty leads him to insist over and over that God alone *really* contemplates himself, that our limited spirit is incapable of grasping the Unlimited Spirit, that his Unlimited Light is too much for us, and that therefore we can say nothing that is worthy of him. The measured gravity of the passages where the pope explores how the divine real-ity encompasses and yet transcends the world are among the more moving expressions of divine transcendence in medieval theology.

"There is no Christian state from which the grace of contemplation can be excluded. Whoever has an interior heart can be illuminated by the light of contemplation."

—Gregory the Great, *Homilies on Ezekiel*

Gregory was concerned with the role of contemplation in the history of salvation. For him, Adam was first and fore-most a contemplative who enjoyed continuous interior loving sight of God. He had been given "inborn firmness of station" (*Mor.* 8.10.19). The fall was caused by Adam turning away from interiority toward the exteriority of sin, and the result was that Adam lost the ability to contemplate. The history of salvation is the history of the stages of contemplation. Bereft of Adam's original inborn firmness, we labor in the toils of the "slippery changeableness" (Mor. 8.10.19) of the sinful world. God became man because of God's loving desire to restore to humanity — even if only partially — Adam's contemplative vision. Christ himself, the Godman, possessed perfect firmness of station, but this gift is not restored to his followers through the grace of redemption. What they gain instead is the firm bond of love found in the church. Therefore, whatever contemplative experience is granted to believers in this life will be less than Adam's — a partial, imperfect, but still precious restoration to what was once enjoyed in paradise.

Contemplation is available to the believing Christian only through Christ, in whom God and humanity are joined. Christ is the necessary center to connect the inner and the outer, contemplation and action, in the present age of salvation. Since the fall, whatever taste of contemplation is restored to us can be effected only through the Godman, who first brings us to faith and then to the possibility of vision. The ability to desire God, lost in the fall, is what Christ's victory over the devil brings back to humanity. "Unless, as we said, the Omnipotent Word became human for the sake of humans, human hearts would not have been able to fly up to contemplate the excellence of the Word" (Hom. on Ez. 1.3.14). Indeed, as a text from the twenty-sixth Homily on the Gospels puts it, the measure of our love for Christ (i.e., the whole Christ) is the yardstick for "how high we ascend to behold the divine omnipotence" (Hom. on the Gospels 26.12). What enables us actually to begin to enjoy contemplation once again as members of the total Christ is the action of the Holy Spirit in our lives. Gregory emphasizes the Spirit's

role as the internal teacher: "Unless the Spirit is present in
the hearer's heart, the teacher's word is useless" (*Hom.* 30.3).
The action of both Christ and the Spirit becomes lively in the
soul through the virtues of faith, hope, and charity, as well
as the effects of the seven gifts of the Holy Spirit (wisdom,
understanding, counsel, fortitude, knowledge, piety, and the
fear of the Lord). Gregory sees the virtues as the means by
which we are led back from our present dispersion in the distractions of the exterior world into the interior realm where
God can be briefly glimpsed (*Hom. on Ez.* 2.5.8–16). The role
of the seven gifts is to deepen and perfect the divine action
that flows into the soul through the virtues.

The role of the Eucharist, for Gregory, is a vital element
in the believer's appropriation of Christ's redeeming activity.
Here the pope's emphasis on the role of suffering in the Christian life meshes with an important transition in early medieval
spirituality that began to consider the Eucharist as sacrifice
more than as an act of thanksgiving. Gregory is still far from
the eucharistic mysticism of the later Middle Ages, but his
stress on the Christian's special access to Christ the Victim
in the Mass, and the corresponding obligation to accept the
role of suffering victim in a fallen world, adumbrates much
that was to come.

Gregory has a good deal to say, though not in a systematic program, about the preparation that the Christian must
engage in to get ready for contemplation, while at the same
time he insists that contemplation is always a divine gift
dependent on God's initiative. The fundamental preparation
for contemplation is, of course, devout living of the Christian life. Gregory considered the active life, fruitful in works
of love of neighbor, as standing in reciprocal relationship

with contemplation: active virtue helps foster more intense contemplation. Gregory also mentioned important specific practices to prepare the believer for the gift of contemplation. These included the reading and study of scripture, as well as the special cultivation of humility, along with other virtues, such as discretion.

However, what Gregory emphasized the most, to such an extent that he often speaks of it as the first stage in the path of contemplation itself, is the necessity for withdrawal from exterior distractions into the interior self, to "call the self back to the self." What really counted for the saint was to turn away from the distractions of knowing about *things* to the serious, even frightening, task of reflecting on the inner self. It is this that leads to the freedom from exterior realities that allows the coals of love for God to be enkindled, "surpassing all mutable things," [so that the heart] "in the very tranquility of its quiet, is in the world but outside it" (*Mor.* 22.16.35).

To realize this goal, Gregory describes three broad stages in the mystical ascent:

> The first step is that one call the self back to the self; the second that one inspects what has been recollected; the third that one rise above the self by giving one's attention over to the contemplation of the invisible Maker. But you cannot recollect yourself unless you have learned to lock out the ghosts of the images of earthly and heavenly things from the mind's eyes. (*Hom. on Ez.* 2.5.9)

Such silence, for Gregory, involves not only canceling the noises of the exterior world, but also cultivating a necessary interior silence, a stillness that is more than just the absence of mundane noise. He is well aware of how hard-won this silence can be:

> Solitude of mind is rightly given at first to those turning
> from the world in order to restrain the clamor of earthly
> desires rising from within and to stifle through the grace
> of supernal love the cares of the heart, boiling over into
> the depths.... It is like chasing away some circling flies
> from the mind's eyes with the hand of seriousness —
> as if they seek a kind of secret within between God
> and themselves where they can silently speak with him
> through internal desires when all outside rumble has
> ceased. (*Mor.* 30.16.52)

Christian belief modified the Greek categories of the active life of the citizen and the contemplative life of the philosopher: the two ways of living became related modalities of the Christian life, active exercise of love toward the neighbor, and the believer's primary intention, unrestricted desire for the vision of God. The relation of contemplation to action was an important question for the monastic pope, as it was for other mystics. Though he affirmed the possibility that the grace of contemplation could be given to both higher and lower clergy and even to the married, it was most frequently given to monks, "those set apart" for the life of contemplation. Gregory, following tradition, considered the contemplative life superior to the active life, yet he worked out in some detail the description of the even higher mixed life of action and contemplation — nothing less than the life of bishops as rulers and preachers.

In his characteristic way, he brings out the interaction between the works of Christian love and contemplative rest from external activity, which allows full interior attention to the presence of God. "By means of the active life we ought to pass to the contemplative, and sometimes, through what we have seen within the mind, the contemplative life should better recall us to the active" (*Hom. on Ez.* 2.2.11). The grounds for this interaction lie in the very nature of contemplative experience itself. Contemplation is a wrestling match with God, as the example of Jacob shows (Gen. 32:22–32) — one in which we can never be on top for long. After a brief moment of contemplative light we will always be quickly cast back into the darkness of our sinful selves. Still, having compassion on our neighbor in the active life is the way to be joined to God in the contemplative.

Though Gregory had great nostalgia for his early monastic life, as bishop of Rome he had been called to the mixed life of contemplation and action. We can see from his writings that for him the monk is the figure of what humanity in Adam was originally created to enjoy: oneness of contemplative attention to God. But even monks no longer live in paradise. Though they exist to remind us of what once was, and better yet, what is to come in heaven, in the present world, whose fallenness Gregory the Great felt so keenly, it is the preacher, living out his perilous vocation to keep both his eye on the goal and his heart with suffering humanity, who is the truest mystic — the contemplative in action, like the great pope himself.

THE RELATION OF
LOVE AND KNOWLEDGE

The relation between love and knowledge in the path to the consciousness of God is one of the essential themes of

Western Christian mysticism. Gregory the Great taught the
necessity for both knowing and loving in the growth of contemplation. It was he who coined the famous phrase *amor
ipse notitia est,* "Love itself is a form of knowledge" (*Hom. on
the Gospels* 27.4), a phrase which summarizes the gist of the
teaching he developed from Augustine and passed on to the
medieval mystics. We need to know God before we can love
God, and that knowing comes through the hearing that is
faith. But faith leads us on to loving consciousness of God in
contemplation, a love that gives us an intuitive knowledge of
God that surpasses all discursive, rational knowing.

Gregory's teaching on love and desire unveils the para-
doxes involved. When we love God as present, we can never
exhaust that presence (and therefore we continue to desire
God), and when we desire God because we perceive his
absence, the very desire itself is a form of presence: "Whoever desires God with the whole mind already has the one
he loves" (*Hom. on the Gospels* 30.1). For Gregory, desire and
love are the language we use to talk to God. Some of his comments on the Song of Songs develop the themes of love and
desire, but perhaps the most erotic passage in all of Gregory's
oeuvre is the description of Mary Magdalene at the tomb
found in Gospel Homily 25. After summarizing the account
of Mary's desperate seeking for Jesus in the tomb inspired by
her burning love, he continues:

> Therefore, first she sought but found not at all. She
> persevered in her seeking and so it came to pass that
> she did find. This was done so that her expanding desires
> might grow and as they grew might take hold of what

they sought. This is why it says of the Lover in the Song of Songs, "On my little bed night after night I sought him whom my soul loves; I sought him and did not find him." (25.2)

Like almost all Christian mystics, Gregory insisted on the priority of love in the mystical path, but he claimed that knowing plays a necessary if subordinate role. The pope left to his successors the problem of trying to explain what kind of knowledge contemplative love actually brings. What he made perfectly clear for them, however, was that knowledge needed love more than love needed knowledge. Longing desire for God would expand and open the mind to heights undreamed of on the human level.

But what exactly is the experience of contemplation, the vision of God? Though his discussions are not autobiographical, we have no doubt that the pope was speaking out of his own experience, especially given his mention of how often he had enjoyed contemplation in his days of monastic quietude. Always, for Gregory, there is the emphasis on interiority and on withdrawal from exterior concerns. In *Moralia* 23.21.40–43 he comments on Job 33:16 ("Then he opened the ears of men and instructed them by discipline"), using the text to bring out an important experience related to the fourth mode of compunction (the piercing we experience when considering where we are not, that is, not in the peace of heaven). This is the experience of relapse, of feeling cast forth from the sweetness of the vision of eternal light to fall back upon our own internal darkness. There is, then, an oscillation from the heights of contemplation to the depths of ourselves, a "beating back" always encountered in trying to contemplate God's overwhelming majesty. The positive side of this relapse experience is that the soul begins to strip away the images of this world that impede it from the ascent. Gregory highlights the value of this oscillation as a discipline to emphasize the necessity for continuing ascetic effort toward the endless possession of the divine vision.

In another text, the comment on Job 33:26b ("He will see his face in jubilation") in *Moralia* 24.6.10–12, Gregory emphasizes the joyful and ineffable nature of mystical consciousness. God draws us on and gladdens us by making himself known to us in the ineffable compunction of love. An inexpressible joy takes place in the mind when one knows what is beyond knowing and yet, since the human consciousness is scarcely able to contemplate it, the human tongue is inadequate to express it.

> *Gregory, following tradition, considered the contemplative life superior to the active life, yet he worked out in some detail the description of the even higher mixed life of action and contemplation.*

Gregory never forgets the needed cleansing that prepares for this experience and the limitations it meets. He reminds us that the fire of tribulation is needed to cleanse the mind before, with the "rust of vices" cleaned away, "it is suddenly illuminated by the bright coruscations of unbounded Light" (*Mor.* 24.6.11). This experience, one of light, of security, of renovation is, however, also an experience of paradox: "The closer it approaches the Truth, the more it knows it is far from it, because had it not beheld it at least in some way it would never have realized that it could not behold it." In one of his most penetrating and moving passages, Gregory says,

> In the very act of directing its intention [to the Truth], the intellectual soul's effort is beaten back by the encircling gleam of its immensity. This Truth fills all things; it encircles all things. Therefore, our minds can never be expanded to comprehend the unbounded encircling, because it is hemmed in by the imperfection of its own bounded existence. (24.16.12)

In the *Homilies on Ezekiel* Gregory anchors his explanation of contemplation both in scriptural archetypes (Moses, Elijah) and in the language of experience. Here he goes beyond the hints he has given elsewhere to emphasize that the fulfillment of all the Old Testament archetypes of contemplation comes in the final reality of Christ, whose saving works and presence in the church enable us, like Elijah, to "long for the King, to desire the citizens we know, and while standing in this edifice of holy church to fix our eyes on the door" (2.1.18). Gregory's mysticism, like that of the other fathers, has a pronounced ecclesiological dimension.

Pope Gregory is known for his light imagery, stunningly evoked in his images of the "chink" and "flash" of contemplation. The first suggests the way in which the Divine Light is restricted by having to pass through a created medium, and the second suggests the subjective experience of the mystic, as when in a darkened room we are suddenly struck by a gleam of light coming through a crack. He is probably speaking of his own experience of the sudden onset and brevity of contemplation when he comments,

> The part through which the light enters is narrow, but the interior part that receives the light is wide because the minds of those contemplating, although they see only a bit of the True Light in tenuous fashion, are still enlarged in themselves to a great breadth: ... Their minds are opened up to an increase of fervor and love, and they become more spacious within so that they admit Truth's Light inside through narrow openings. (*Hom. on Ez.* 2.5.17)

Characteristically Gregorian, however, is the experience of darkness — even of terror — that follows close on the joy of light. The terror is real for him. The frightening recognition of personal sinfulness and fear of God seems to have been a necessary concomitant to all his contemplative experiences. Not only that, but the person gifted with contemplation is especially vulnerable to temptation, in particular the temptation to pride in having reached these spiritual heights. Again we see Gregory's theme of oscillation: "By compunction or contemplation they are raised up to God, but the weight of their temptation beats them back upon themselves, so that temptation weighs them down lest contemplation puff them up, and likewise contemplation raises them lest temptation sink them" (*Hom. on Ez.* 2.2.3). The mutual interaction between the joy and peace given in contemplation and the sting of the flesh present in temptation is a special note of Gregory's teaching. He is no doubt reflecting on aspects of his own suffering within the joys of contemplation.

CONCLUSION

Though the world and the culture of Gregory the Great are far removed from our own, we cannot help being moved by the struggles of this man, a leader deeply involved with terrible social and political upheavals, who, pierced with the wound of distraction, fights for the life of silence, interiority, and contemplation. In our own distressed world, we can well appreciate the difficulties of brushing away the flies of distraction from the eyes of the mind. We are also touched by the insistence from this monastic pope on the availability of contemplation for all who seek the presence of God — including the married: "There is no Christian state from which the grace of contemplation can be excluded. Whoever has an interior heart can be illuminated by the light of contemplation . . . so that no one might glory in this grace as a private possession" (*Hom. on Ez.* 2.5.19). Across the centuries the lugubrious Gregory the Great, "Doctor of Desire," reaches us with hope and encouragement.

SUGGESTIONS FOR FURTHER READING

There is no adequate anthology of Gregory's voluminous writings. An early nineteenth-century translation of his masterpiece, the *Morals on Job,* exists, but it is hard to find and harder to read. Among the translations of other works, see St. Gregory the Great, *Pastoral Care,* translated by Henry Davis, Ancient Christian Writers 11 (New York: Paulist Press, 1950); St. Gregory the Great, *Dialogues,* translated by Odo John Zimmerman, Fathers of the Church 39 (Washington, D.C.: Catholic University Press, 1959); Gregory the

Great, *Forty Gospel Homilies,* translated by Dom David Hurst (Kalamazoo, Mich.: Cistercian Publications, 1990); and *The Homilies of Saint Gregory the Great on the Book of the Prophet Ezekiel,* translated by Theodosia Gray (Etna, Calif.: Center for Traditionalist Orthodox Studies, 1990). Important English works on Gregory include Carole Straw, *Gregory the Great: Perfection in Imperfection* (Berkeley: University of California Press, 1988); John C. Cavadini, ed., *Gregory the Great: A Symposium* (Notre Dame, Ind.: University of Notre Dame Press, 1995); and R. A. Markus, *Gregory the Great and His World* (Cambridge: Cambridge University Press, 1997).

Five

Vision and Authority

HILDEGARD OF BINGEN

LIFE

"God chose the lowly and despised of the world, and those who count for nothing, to reduce to nothing those who are something, so that no human being might boast before God" (1 Cor. 1:28–29). With this text as warrant, Hildegard of Bingen and other female seers of the Middle Ages, such as Mechthild of Madgeburg, Birgitta of Sweden, and Joan of Arc, claimed their status as voices of reform and prophets of both coming events and the end times. Using the reversal of values announced in the scriptural text, Hildegard,

97

as a "weak woman," was fearless in challenging the abuses and failures of twelfth-century prelates, calling on them to cleanse the church and the clergy in the shadow of the Second Coming. Nor did she spare secular authorities who abused their power. Hildegard's influence as visionary and prophet came from the accepted belief that in times of crisis, when male leadership failed, God could inspire women to take up his work. Churchmen at the highest level, including Pope Eugene III and (more cautiously) Bernard of Clairvaux, certified that her gifts of vision and prophecy were God-given.

Hildegard was born in 1098, the youngest of ten children of a noble family. When she was eight years old her parents gave her to be the companion of Jutta, a noblewoman only six years older. Jutta was determined to pursue a severe ascetic religious life. In 1112 Jutta, along with Hildegard and a few other young girls, took monastic vows at the male monastery of St. Disibod. Here Hildegard received her education under Jutta's tutelage, but she did not follow Jutta's extreme asceticism, keeping instead to the moderation advised in the Benedictine rule. When Jutta died at forty-four, Hildegard was elected to lead the group, which continued to grow. In time Hildegard became prioress of the women and lobbied for their independence from the monastery of St. Disibod. She won the struggle to establish a separate monastery for her women on the height called Rupertsberg opposite the town of Bingen at the confluence of the Rhine and Nahe rivers.

Hildegard had experienced visions from childhood, but a crisis came for her when she was forty-three. She saw a "great splendor" and heard a voice from heaven commanding her to write down "what you see and hear." Though

encouraged by Volmar, the monk who served as her secre-
tary and confidant, she was still terrified of the task to the
point of becoming seriously ill. Eventually she overcame her
fears and began to write. She emerged as a powerful visionary,
the "Sibyl of the Rhine." During the 1140s, Hildegard began
an extensive program of letter writing to popes, emperors,
bishops, theologians, indeed, all classes of Christian society.
Her growing reputation as someone inspired by God meant
that many people turned to her, not only to answer theological questions, but also for personal advice. Hildegard's
almost four hundred surviving letters illustrate an important
function of medieval saints, that of providing living proof that
God was not distant or indifferent, but was actively involved
in people's lives through his chosen instruments.

Even more extraordinary was Hildegard's public activity,
something virtually unprecedented for a woman. She undertook four extensive public preaching journeys late in life: the
first along the river Main (1158–59); a second to Lorraine in
1160; a third down the Rhine between 1161 and 1163; and
a final trip through Swabia (1167–70). During these travels she preached in many of the main cities of Germany,
announcing the need for reform and proclaiming a warning of divine wrath to come. An example of her message
can be found in a famous sermon given at Cologne in 1163,
which denounced the clergy for the vices and pastoral negligence that had allowed the Cathar heresy to infect their
flock. Hildegard's message was uncompromising: "Because of
your wicked deeds, which are devoid of light, God will wreak
his vengeance upon you, and he will be so hidden in that
vengeance that you will have no hope of deliverance." She
concludes on a personal note: "Poor little timorous figure of

a woman that I am, I have worn myself out for two whole years so that I might bring this message in person to the magistrates, teachers, and other wise men who hold the higher positions in the church" (Letter 15). When Hildegard died in 1179 she was famous throughout Europe. In later centuries her reputation waxed and waned. In the early twentieth century the Vatican approved her cult as a saint for Germany; in recent decades she is being appreciated as one of the most remarkable women in the history of Christianity. Hildegard was unique in the way in which she combined the offices of visionary, mystic, prophet, and apocalyptic reformer.

WRITINGS AND THEOLOGY

It was unusual, but not unknown, for women to become writers in the early Middle Ages. The fact that Hildegard made use of secretaries to help compose her Latin works does not detract from her status as an author: most male monastics also used secretaries to help in the process of composition. The idiosyncratic nature of Hildegard's Latin itself proclaims the distinctiveness of her thought and style. What is especially astonishing about Hildegard's corpus is its diversity. This German nun was universal in her interests, a true renaissance figure — not only the first major female theologian, but also a poet, composer, preacher, playwright, scientist, and medical author, especially on topics relating to female sexuality and gynecology. The hymns in her *Symphony of the Harmony of Celestial Revelations* place her in the forefront of medieval composers; her *Order of the Virtues* is the earliest extant morality play. The centerpiece of her production, however, rests in the great theological trilogy comprised of the *Scivias* (*Know the Ways of the Lord*, 1141–51), the *Liber vitae meritorum* (*Book of the Rewards of Life*, 1158–63), and the *Liber divinorum operum* (*Book of Divine Works*, 1163–73). The first and last of these works come equipped with illustrations of the visions that were the basis for her lengthy theological exposition. While debate continues about how far these pictures go back to Hildegard herself, most authorities consider her to be among the first theologians to commission illustrations as an integral aspect of their theology.

To highlight the nature of Hildegard's contribution to theology we can consider her writings from the perspective of three broad categories of medieval theology. The best-known form of medieval theology is the scholastic model, the professional and academic "faith seeking understanding," born in the twelfth century and proliferating in universities through the sixteenth century and beyond. During the past half-century, recognition has been given to the monastic theology developed among the followers of Benedict that reached its culmination in the twelfth century among the Cistercians. In recent years, students of the Middle Ages have begun to recognize a third strand, what can be called vernacular theology, produced by those who had not had university educations, but who had read widely and pondered deeply on how to understand the faith and present it to others. Vernacular theology was most often set forth in the native tongue, and many of its most famous proponents were women, such as the Dutch beguine Hadewijch (ca. 1250), the Italian third-order Dominican Catherine of Siena (d. 1380), and the English anchoress Julian of Norwich (d. ca. 1416). Hildegard of Bingen is unique in being a female monastic theologian, not a vernacular theologian. All her works are in Latin, and her world was formed by the traditions of monastic theology, though she adapted them for her own purposes.

Monastic theology was essentially exegetical in method, salvation-historical in scope, and contemplative in its goal. If "I believe so that I may understand" can be said to be the predominant motif of scholastic theology, then "I believe so that I may experience" has been identified as the guiding aim of monastic theology. Like that of other monastics, Hildegard's theology was exegetical, universal, and experiential, though expressed very much in her own voice. As a woman, Hildegard had not been given professional training in Latin and in scriptural exegesis. Hence, she never wrote formal biblical commentaries, as did her male monastic counterparts such as Rupert of Deutz, Bernard of Clairvaux, and Joachim of Fiore.

Rather than the Bible, it is Hildegard's visions, another form of direct message from God, that serve as the base text for the commentarial theology that allows her to set forth her message. This is not to deny that Hildegard had deep insight into the spiritual sense of the Bible. There is an interesting progress evident in her trilogy. The two early works, the *Scivias* and the *Book of the Rewards of Life,* tend to use scripture piecemeal, citing individual proof texts to confirm the interpretation of the visions. By the time she had come to write her last work, however, Hildegard's visionary authority had empowered her to insert into her visionary account long commentaries on two of the most difficult texts of scripture, the creation narrative of Genesis and the prologue to John's Gospel.

Hildegard, like the other great monastic theologians, was not concerned with the scientific distinction and logical analysis of various doctrines; she remained focused on the totality of salvation history. The story of redemption is rooted in God's trinitarian life, that is, the revelation of the Trinity as the mystery of creative love. Her presentation of the message of salvation deals fundamentally with creation, fall, and the return to God made possible through the coming of the Godman and his ongoing presence in the church. Hildegard's trilogy takes up these issues and their many implications.

The *Scivias* comprises twenty-four visions divided into three books. Each chapter contains a picture of the vision, a brief prose description, and a longer exegesis of its meaning. The topics are not laid out in any logical order, but book 1 deals primarily with cosmology and the fall, while book 2 concerns human formation, the Trinity, and the role of the church and its sacraments. The long book 3 contains visions relating to Christ, the church, the virtues, and the last times. The *Book of the Rewards of Life* is an ethical handbook on sin and virtue divided into six parts. It does not provide a picture of the cosmic winged man that is its visionary basis, but the image is described at some length in the text. Finally, the *Book of Divine Works* contains ten illustrated visions broken down into three parts. Part 1 again deals with the Trinity and cosmology. Part 2 has a single vision of the earth divided into five zones, which Hildegard uses to expose a cosmology based on her original exegesis of the Genesis creation account as figuring both the life of the church and the inner life of each human. Part 3 has five visions of the building of the City of God.

The twelfth century was an age of renewal of interest in trinitarian theology, as well as in cosmology and in the church's role in the ages of history leading to the Second Coming. These concerns are evident in Hildegard's distinctive thought. Hildegard's doctrine of God stresses the activity

of the three-personed God in history more than the exploration of the inner life of the Trinity. In presenting this
doctrine, the German nun often makes use of feminine images
to manifest the divine action, particularly the Divine Wisdom
(*Sapientia*) in which God formed all things and continues to
direct them down to the end of time. Vision 9 of book 3
of the *Scivias* describes Wisdom as "the great ornament of
God and the broad stairway of all the other virtues that live
in him, joined to him in sweet embrace in a dance of ardent
love." Hildegard's cosmology and eschatology are original and
complex and cannot be taken up here.

---

*"Heaven was opened and a fiery light of the
greatest brilliance came down and filled my
whole head, my whole heart, and my whole
breast, like a flame not so much burning as
warming."* — Hildegard of Bingen, *Scivias*

Finally, we can ask to what degree Hildegard's theology
was contemplative and mystical. Here we confront an initial paradox. Like all monastic authors, the German nun
often spoke of contemplation; but, unlike her contemporaries,
such as Bernard of Clairvaux, William of St. Thierry, and
even the quasi-monastic Richard of St. Victor, Hildegard did
not lay out programs of mystical practice and contemplation
designed to lead to deeper personal experience of the Bridegroom of the Song of Songs, or to perceiving the action of
the Trinity in the depths of the soul. When she speaks of
"mystical mysteries" and "mystical words," she is referring to

the hidden meanings of the scriptural text. From this perspective, Hildegard is not a mystic in the sense of the other twelfth-century authors treated here. The dominant motifs in her life are those of the reformer, the artist, and the prophet. And yet there are important mystical aspects in Hildegard. Bernard of Clairvaux is not less a mystic because he was also a church reformer. Hildegard is primarily a prophet, but she is also of significance for the history of mysticism for the ways in which she used an appeal to visionary authority to ground her message.

VISIONS AND AUTHORITY

Augustine of Hippo laid down the basis for the medieval theory of visions in the last book of his *Literal Commentary on Genesis* (see chapter 8 below). Visions could be either corporeal, spiritual (i.e., in the imagination), or purely intellectual. The bishop's concern was primarily with sorting out how God communicated with humans in scripture, but he put no limit on God's ongoing ability to manifest himself to others in the course of history. When it came to the authority to be accorded to visionary claims made by contemporaries, Augustine followed Paul (see 1 Cor. 12:10) in emphasizing the need for the discernment of spirits to determine the difference between the true and the false.

Prior to the twelfth century, mystics rarely made direct appeal to their own experiences of God, visionary or not, to ground their message. The autobiographical vein was not their métier. The situation began to change in the twelfth century, as we see in the case of Hildegard. This age witnessed the onset of a visionary explosion that became more and more evident in the later Middle Ages. The nature of visions also began to shift. The form of vision that flourished between the sixth and the early twelfth centuries stressed a journey to heaven and/or hell, usually unique and of considerable duration. During this rapture, the visionary, often a sinner or indifferent Christian, experienced a conversion that he or she used as a warning to others after the return to normal consciousness. A second type of vision began in the twelfth century and became predominant in subsequent ages. This was a brief, repeatable experience, less concerned with general conversion and the threat of judgment (though these could be present) than with the manifestation of a heavenly figure who imparts a particular message to the seer.

The effect the showing had upon the visionary, as well as the type of message given, could be quite varied. Many of these messages were concerned with the political and ecclesiastical problems of the day; others were individual communications of approbation or reprobation. Such visions are better thought of as prophetic and reforming rather than as mystical. Mystical visions, on the other hand, emphasize a transformative contact with God that provides the recipient with ineffable knowledge and frequently with a sense of deep union. Some, though not all, of Hildegard's showings fit this category. While the teaching found in her trilogy is primarily theological, cosmological, and eschatological in the broad sense, her visionary persona and the authority she claims for her teaching are in large part mystical. In this sense she is a prototype of many of the mystical women of the later Middle Ages. Hildegard is also unique for her "visionology," that is, the way in which she sought to describe and analyze the modalities of the showings God sent her.

Hildegard was famed as a visionary. Her biographer, the monk Theodorich of Echternach, says, "The mode of vision found in this holy virgin was truly marvelous and exceedingly rare" (*Life of St. Hildegard* I.viii). Hildegard's forms of visionary experience stretch the Augustinian categories almost to the breaking point. So detailed are her accounts of how her visions came to her that some have seen evidence that the more pictorial visualizations indicate she suffered from a form of migraine headache.

From the age of five Hildegard tells us that she experienced a state of constant, nonecstatic vision, which coexisted with her ordinary modes of consciousness. She described these manifestations in a letter to Guibert of Gembloux in 1175:

> In this vision my spirit ascends into the height of the firmament and the changing air, and it spreads itself abroad among diverse peoples though they are in distant regions and places removed from me. And because I see these things in such a manner, I therefore also behold them in changing forms of clouds and other creatures. But I do not hear them with my bodily ears, nor with my heart's thoughts, nor do I perceive them by using any of my five senses, but only in my soul, with my outer eyes open, so that I never experience their failure in ecstasy. Rather, I see these things wide-awake, day and night. (Letter 103r)

Hildegard continues: "The brightness that I see is not spatial, yet it is far, far more lucent than a cloud that envelops the sun. I cannot contemplate height or length or breadth in it; and I call it the reflection of the living light." In, or perhaps better on, this bright shadow, as if projected on a movie screen, Hildegard tells us that she sees and hears the things she reveals in her writings:

> As the sun, moon, and stars appear mirrored in water, so writings, discourses, virtues, and certain human works are formed and flash forth for me in this light.... And the things I write are those I see and hear through the vision.... And the words that I see and hear in the vision are not like words that come from human lips, but like a sparkling flame and a cloud moved in pure air.

It is this nonecstatic vision projected on the inner senses, something she at times refers to as a "mystic vision" (i.e., one hidden within), that forms the basis for her trilogy. These pictures often came accompanied by auditions in which a divine voice explained a point or issued a warning. However original such visions were both in content and mode of reception, contemporaries would have placed them under Augustine's category of spiritual vision.

At some point in her life another, more rare and mystical form of vision began. She describes this with greater difficulty in the letter to Guibert:

> And in that same light I sometimes, not often, see another light, which I call "the Living Light." How I see it I can say much less about than with the case of the former light; and while I am gazing at it all sadness and all pain is taken from me, so that I am like an innocent young girl and not an old woman. (Letter 103r)

This mode of seeing did not involve images or pictures, and it seems to be associated with the influx of divine light and fire she received in 1141. "Heaven was opened and a fiery light of the greatest brilliance came down and filled my whole head, my whole heart, and my whole breast, like a flame not so much burning as warming" (*Scivias*, prologue). In a letter she wrote to Bernard of Clairvaux in 1147, she earlier attempted to describe the nature of this illumination that granted her intuitive knowledge of the meaning of the Bible. Hildegard said:

> Through this vision that touches my heart and soul like a burning flame, teaching me profundities of meaning, I have an inward understanding of the Psalter, the Gospels, and other volumes. Nevertheless, I do not receive this knowledge in German. Indeed, I have no formal training for it, for I know how to read on only the most elementary level, certainly with no deep analysis. (Letter 1)

This showing does not involve a visualizable form. Hildegard describes this contact in terms of its transformative effects on herself, the inner joy and rejuvenation it brings. Above all, it gives her miraculous and comprehensive knowledge of the inner meaning of scripture. This gift is of central importance for her authority as a theologian. Lacking the formal training denied her as a woman, it was essential that she have such a claim to divine authorization for interpreting the scriptures.

In the seventh vision recounted in a section from her lost autobiography that survives due to its inclusion in the *Life of St. Hildegard*, the prioress gives a description of a vision from around 1167 that is also distinctively mystical in character and once again related to the Bible. She says:

Finally, in the time that followed I saw a mystic and wondrous vision, such that my insides were convulsed and my body's power of sensation was extinguished, because my knowledge was transmuted to another mode as if I did not know myself. And from God's inspiration, as it were, drops of sweet rain splashed into my soul's knowledge, just as the Holy Spirit filled John the Evangelist when he sucked supremely deep revelation from the breast of Jesus, when his understanding was so touched by holy divinity that he revealed hidden mysteries and works, saying, "In the beginning was the Word." (*Life* II.xvi)

Two things stand out about this account: first, its ecstatic nature, so different from Hildegard's usual mode of vision; and second, its relationship to an intuitive grasp of divine mysteries similar to that expressed by John in the prologue to his Gospel. What the nun is claiming here is that she has enjoyed the same direct contact with the Word that John, the mystical Gospel writer, also had. John was the ideal role model for Hildegard's revelations, because he had received both spiritual visions, as evidenced in the Apocalypse, and the higher intellectual vision: the intuitive grasp of the Divine Word accorded to him when he rested his head on the bosom of Jesus (see John 13:23). Hildegard saw herself as a female version of the Beloved Disciple.

When Hildegard expounds the mystical insight she was given into the teaching of the Word, she emphasizes its universal character, much like John the Scot (see chapter 10 below), whose writings she appears to have had some contact with, whether directly or through intermediaries. This is

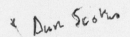

evident in her commentary on the Johannine prologue (John 1:1–14) found in vision 4 of part 1 of the *Book of Divine Works*. Hildegard shows little interest in the inner relations of the Trinity; her concern is cosmic, that is, how the Father expresses himself through the Son in order to make all things. As she puts it: "And why is the Word spoken? Because with the sound of his voice he called forth all creatures and called them to himself" (*Book* 1.4.105). The main concern of both her commentary on John's prologue and that on the creation account of Genesis that comes later in this work is an insistence on what can be called a "pan-Christic" ontology, that is, the teaching that when the Father calls forth the world through the Son he does so precisely that the Word may become man.

> *Today Hildegard of Bingen's music sounds on the airways, her morality play has been performed for the first time in eight centuries, her art is reproduced and admired, and her herbal and medical writings are mined as resources for alternative medicine.*

John's prologue, according to Hildegard, reveals three essential truths. First, the meaning of creation as divine theophany, or manifestation of all that pre-existed in the Word from all eternity. Hildegard says: "When the Word of God sounded, it called to itself every creature that had been preordained and established by God in primordial time, and through its voice it aroused all to life" (*Book* 1.4.105). Second, the prologue teaches humanity's function as the microcosmic focus of the universe. Humanity can glory in this role because its share in divine "reason" (*rationalitas*) enables humans to embrace all things in their knowing (a reminiscence of Eriugena). It is for this reason that the prologue reveals the third truth, namely, that the act of creation in and through the Word necessarily finds its purpose and completion in the Word's taking on flesh. Hildegard proclaims this interpretation in God's own voice:

> And so I composed the small work which is humanity in myself and made it according to my image and likeness, so that it might work in anything whatever according to me. This is because my Son was to be clothed in humanity with a garment of flesh. I set up humanity as a rational reality from my own rationality, and placed my own power in it, just as the rationality of humanity in its talent embraces all things through name and number. (*Book* 1.4.105)

CONCLUSION

Today Hildegard of Bingen's music sounds on the airways, her morality play has been performed for the first time in eight centuries, her art is reproduced and admired, and her herbal and medical writings are mined as resources for alternative medicine. This rediscovery of the redoubtable German nun is fitting recognition for one of the most remarkable figures of the Middle Ages. Even those who have never received direct showings from God can appreciate the mystical roots of Hildegard's profound theology. Despite the time-bound and culturally specific aspects of her message, we sense the inner truth of what she proclaims in Letter 52 when she says, "These words do not come from a human being, but from the Living Light; let the one who hears see and believe where these words come from."

SUGGESTIONS FOR FURTHER READING

For a translation of Hildegard's longest work, see *Hildegard of Bingen: Scivias*, translated by Columba Hart and Jane Bishop, Classics of Western Spirituality (New York: Paulist Press, 1990). There is also a version of the second book in her trilogy, *Hildegard of Bingen: The Book of the Rewards of Life*, translated by Bruce W. Hozeski (New York: Oxford University Press, 1994). Unfortunately, only a partial and unreliable version exists of the third book, *Hildegard of Bingen's Book of Divine Works*, edited by Matthew Fox (Santa Fe, N.Mex.: Bear & Co., 1987). Many other works of Hildegard are now available, including *The Letters of Hildegard of Bingen*, translated by Joseph L. Baird and Radd K. Ehrman, 2 vols. (New York: Oxford University Press, 1994–98); and *The Life of the Holy Hildegard by the Monks Gottfried and Theodoric*, translated by Adelgundis Führkötter (Collegeville, Minn.: Liturgical Press, 1995). For an overview of Hildegard's many contributions, see Barbara Newman, ed., *Voice of the Living Light: Hildegard of Bingen and Her World* (Berkeley: University of California Press, 1998). Among other studies, see Barbara Newman, *Sister of Wisdom: St. Hildegard's Theology of the Feminine* (Berkeley: University of California Press, 1987); and Sabina Flanagin, *Hildegard of Bingen, 1098–1179: A Visionary Life* (New York: Routledge, 1989).

Six

Modes of Contemplation

RICHARD OF ST. VICTOR

LIFE

Richard of St. Victor lived and worked within the context of a monasticized way of life for priests developed in the eleventh and twelfth centuries. Living a communal life under a version of the Rule St. Augustine had established for priests living with him in the bishop's residence, these "canons regular" established canonical houses — some in rural areas, but others in urban environments with an emphasis on pastoral service. In 1108 the learned Parisian master of theology

William of Champeaux retired from the episcopal school of
that city to found a house of canons at the hermitage of
St. Victor outside the city walls. A school was formed there,
which became one of the most renowned educational insti-
tutions of the twelfth century. The house was made a royal
abbey by King Louis VI. The fame of the School of St. Victor
is due to the noted teacher Hugh, who entered the community around 1120 and died in 1141. Richard of St. Victor
came later and may not have studied with Hugh but can certainly be called an indirect disciple of the famous master. We
know almost nothing about Richard's life except that he was
born in Scotland and that he served as teaching master at
the school and then as sub-prior and prior of the house of
St. Victor before his death on March 10, 1173.

The Victorines were major proponents of the new development in theology at Paris that came to be known as
scholasticism. Scholasticism explored the possibility of a
"scientific" model of theology that not only offered the
opportunity to work out carefully distinguished theological
operations designed for specific tasks, but also called for new
thought about how theology related to other forms of knowledge and how to present the teaching of theology according
to proper scientific and pedagogical requirements. In essence,
scholastic theology refers to an original modality, a new
method, approach, or set of operations for appropriating faith.
As a novel approach to the understanding of faith, it dif-
fered in method from the monastic forms of theology that
had until then dominated the field. Though monastics could
be said to work under the motto, "I believe in order to experience," and scholastics under the motto, "I believe in order

to understand," both agreed in the ultimate purpose of all theological work: to increase love of God and neighbor.

The canons of St. Victor, formed in the intellectual world of Parisian scholastic theology, made notable contributions to twelfth-century mysticism. Although Hugh was the fountainhead of Victorine mysticism, Richard of St. Victor must be counted as the most significant of the Victorine mystics, both for the profundity of his thought and his subsequent influence on the later Western tradition.

WRITINGS

Richard was a prolific writer, responsible for a massive handbook of biblical education called the *Book of Selections*, important scriptural commentaries, and many treatises. His work *On the Trinity* best demonstrates the originality of his theological vision. Richard's mystical teaching is present in many of his writings, but we shall primarily study three of them: the *Twelve Patriarchs*, the *Mystical Ark*, and the *Four Degrees of Violent Charity*. The *Twelve Patriarchs* (often called *Benjamin minor* or the *Preparation of the Intellectual Soul for Contemplation*), interprets the story of Jacob, his wives, concubines, and twelve sons (Gen. 29–35) as a teaching about how the various aspects of knowing and loving prepare the soul for contemplative experience. The *Mystical Ark*, also called *Benjamin major*, or the *Grace of Contemplation*, allegorizes the Ark of the Covenant (Exod. 25) as the master symbol describing the various forms of contemplation. The *Four Degrees of Violent Charity* sketches an itinerary of how vehement love leads to union with God and more perfect service of neighbor, joining the new language of courtly eroticism to the ancient theme of the relation of contemplation and action. Among Richard's most valuable contributions is the psychological penetration that he brings to his ordering of Christian teaching on contemplation.

In continuity with the Cistercians and his Victorine predecessors, Richard's theological anthropology sees the human soul as made to the divine image in its rational-intellectual capacity and to the divine likeness in its ability to love. Though both powers have been damaged by sin, they can be restored, at least to some degree, in this life. Richard's treatises combine the practical and the theoretical aspects of the spiritual work that prepares the soul for immediate contact with God, nourishes the experience itself, and enhances its effects.

THE PATH TO CONTEMPLATION

In the *Twelve Patriarchs* Richard uses the characters in the story of Jacob, whose name became Israel ("the one who sees God"), his two wives, Leah and Rachel, and the twelve sons they and their handmaids bore him, as an elaborate allegory to illustrate how the affective and intellectual powers of the soul are to be trained in the practice of virtue in order to attain contemplation. Benjamin, the last and youngest of the patriarchs, is the figure of the contemplative, intellectual soul. Despite the strains a modern reader feels in reading Richard's personification allegory, where each step in spiritual progress is personified by one of the characters from Genesis, the treatise displays a subtle understanding of the psychology of progress in the spiritual life. The purpose of the treatise is to come to know Benjamin, that is, ecstatic contemplation, at least by knowledge through teaching, if not by higher personal experience.

The spiritual soul (Jacob) cannot immediately enjoy the relationship with the beautiful Rachel that produces Benjamin. First, Jacob must undergo the laborious work of acquiring the virtues symbolized by his marriage with Leah. Her first four children signify the basis for the soul's journey to ecstasy in reforming the affective part of the soul. The journey begins with (1) fear of punishment (Ruben), moves to (2) the grief of penance (Simeon), then on to (3) the hope of forgiveness (Levi), and finally to (4) the love of justice (Judah). Then Rachel's maid Bala, signifying the garrulous imagination who serves as reason's handmaid, comes to the soul's assistance, helping to order our thoughts, since contemplation must begin from images formed in the mind. The birth of Dan (5) to Bala symbolizes reason ordering the images of material things; her second son, Naphtali (6), represents reason rising from material things to the understanding of spiritual things. This involves a form of initial and nonecstatic contemplation.

Zelpha, indicating sensation, is the handmaid of Leah, the soul's power of attracting or willing. Zelpha's union with Jacob produces Gad, the "rigor of abstinence" (7), and Asher, the "vigor of patience" (8). These provide the soul with the strength it needs to practice the obedience that will lead it on to contemplation. But before true contemplation occurs, the power of attraction (Leah) must give birth to two further virtues. Issachar (9), the joy of interior sweetness, is a spiritual gift that belongs to what we might call the contemplative continuum — ranging from spiritual inebriation

THE TWELVE PATRIARCHS
Richard of St. Victor

LEAH: (attraction/desire for justice) seven children representing the "ordered affections"

1. Ruben (fear of punishment)

2. Simeon (grief of penance)

3. Levi (hope of forgiveness)

4. Judah (love of justice)

BALA: Rachel's maid (imagination)

5. Dan (images of material things)

6. Naphtali (images of spiritual things)

ZELPHA: Leah's maid (sense knowing)

7. Gad (abstinence)

8. Asher (patience)

LEAH: second set of offspring

9. Issachar (joy of interior sweetness)

10. Zabulon (hatred of vices)

Interlude:

(a) Dina (ordered shame) is raped by Sichem (love of vainglory), son of Emor (love of self-excellence).

(b) Sichem is murdered by Simeon and Levi (bad spiritual advice)

RACHEL: (reason/pursuit of wisdom) two children

11. Joseph (discretion)

12. Benjamin (contemplative ecstasy)

to St. Paul's being rapt to the third heaven. Zabulon (10), the last of Leah's sons, represents firm hatred of vices, what Richard calls "ordered hatred."

The soul has still not reached the heights of true ecstatic contemplation, however. The next process is represented by the story of Dina, Leah's daughter, who stands for "ordered shame." This shame is not the external shamefacedness we feel before other people for some fault or error, but the internal judgment by which conscience accuses us because of our continuing sinfulness. Dina was raped by Sichem. Allegorically this shows what happens when one lets shame leave its interior home to compare its spiritual status with others, running the risk of being defiled by vainglory over one's own gifts. Sichem was murdered by Simeon and Levi, signifying the bad spiritual advice by which grief and hope for forgiveness exacerbate the fall by their lack of discretion.

This crisis sets up the necessity for the intellectual virtue that plays the decisive role in Richard's path to contemplation — discretion, symbolized by Joseph (11), regulates the interaction of all the prior stages to attune the soul for achieving ecstatic contemplation. Discretion, Rachel's first child, is true self-knowledge, or the fruit of such self-knowledge. "Believe me," says our Victorine, "the intellectual soul makes no more tortuous demand on itself than to preserve the right measure in all its attractions" (*Twelve Patriarchs*, chap. 69). Ultimately reason, personified by Rachel, dies giving birth to Benjamin (12, contemplative ecstasy). Thus it is that only after laborious progress through the virtues and disciplines of the imagination and the body that reason, with divine aid, may finally harmonize fallen humanity for the experience of God that is the final goal.

The intellectual soul, as the "foremost and principal mirror for seeing God," has now polished its clouded surface sufficiently so that, by gazing intently within, a flash of divine light begins to appear in it that enkindles ardent desire for seeing God himself. This light is always a gift of grace, though it comes only to souls who have made intense efforts to attain it. "Benjamin is born and Rachel dies, because when the human mind is rapt above itself all the limits of human reasoning are surpassed. Every form of human reason succumbs to what it beholds of the divine light when it is lifted above itself and rapt in ecstasy" (*Twelve Patriarchs*, chap. 73).

In a final section on the Transfiguration of Christ Richard concludes the treatise by highlighting that it is only in and through the work of Christ that the ascent to the vision of light can be achieved. The three disciples that accompany Christ up the mountain are interpreted as the triple effort that leads to self-knowledge: the effort of works; the effort of meditation; and the effort of prayer. When these three fall on their faces at the sound of the divine voice proclaiming, "This is my Beloved Son in whom I am well pleased" (Matt. 17:5–6), Richard reads this as the failure of all human memory, sense, and reason at the revelation of the incommunicable mystery of the Trinity's unity of substance in diversity of persons.

MODES OF CONTEMPLATION

In the *Mystical Ark* Richard develops his teaching on contemplation into the most complete treatment of the twelfth century. Combining the scholastic and monastic modes of theology by integrating biblical symbolism and mystical speculation, he bases his presentation on the biblical symbol of the encounter with God, namely, the construction of the Ark of the Covenant. The Victorine saw this treatise as addressed to multiple audiences. Book 1 is a brief summary to satisfy busy academic readers; but the rest of the treatise (books 2–5) was written "about contemplation in the manner of a contemplative and the tone of contemplation" (*Mystical Ark* 1.12). This is especially evident in his continuing appeal to personal experience. This typically monastic theme culminates in the final chapter, where Richard abruptly closes off an explanation of Paul's famous rapture (2 Cor. 12) by appealing to the skill of those who have come to the fullness of knowledge "through their own experience more than someone else's teaching" (*Mystical Ark* 5.19). Did Richard himself share in such experience? Given the fact that he compares himself with those who "sweat" to build the Ark rather than to those who enter into it, and that he insists that "few" rise up to the final two levels of contemplation, perhaps he did not. Nevertheless, we are indebted to his teaching on contemplation, the fullest construction of the entire early mystical tradition.

"Believe me, the intellectual soul makes no more tortuous demand on itself than to preserve the right measure in all its attractions."

— Richard of St. Victor, *Twelve Patriarchs*

Like his master Hugh, Richard utilizes a key Old Testament account as the master symbol for describing how fallen humans return to God. The tabernacle described in Exodus

26 that serves as an outer approach to the Ark is the state of perfection or discipline of mind; the courtyard in Exodus 27 that surrounds the tabernacle is the discipline of the body. Richard distinguishes between an exterior tabernacle signifying return to the self and an interior one symbolizing passage beyond the self in contemplation. The Ark of the Covenant itself (Exodus 25) signifies the grace of contemplation, which Richard defines as "the free penetration of the mind, hovering in wonder, into the manifestations of Wisdom" (*Mystical Ark* 1.4).

Richard delineates six forms of contemplation, figured in the six wings of the cherubim by which we are suspended above earthly things and lifted to heavenly ones. The six forms of contemplation involve the three powers of knowing of the immaterial soul: imagination, reason, and understanding. First there is the level of *imagination*, directed (1) to visible things, where we come to admire the Creator on the basis of a consideration of his works. This leads (2) to ideas of visible things, when we move on to consider the inner meanings of these visible things. Then *reason* begins to apprehend (3) the qualities of invisible things and not just their existence as distinct from visible ones. It is here that divine illumination first becomes active in some existential way. In the next level (4) contemplation is symbolically presented in the throne of mercy, the area between the two cherubim on top of the Ark. "From that throne of mercy, between the two cherubs that stand over the ark and its records, my voice shall come to thee" (Exod. 25:22). In this stage imagination has withdrawn and reason operates in itself but already under the influence of the higher power of *understanding*. This is the stage in which

the soul through self-knowledge, that is, through consideration of itself as made in the image and likeness of God, begins
to make the transition to truly mystical contemplation. The
necessity for self-knowledge is stressed again and again, since
this is the means by which a person ascends to contemplation
of the things of heaven. The final two levels of contemplation
take place in *understanding*, which is directed (5) to God as
one, and finally (6) to the Trinity. Richard admonishes that
anyone who wishes to attain the height of knowledge must
be familiar with these six kinds of contemplation.

The last three stages of contemplation are interrelated,
because in the task of faith seeking understanding, we draw
our similitudes for understanding and expressing divine things
primarily from the rational spirit made to God's image and
likeness. We must always remember that in finding likenesses
for the Trinity "the dissimilarity is greater than the similarity"
(*Mystical Ark* 4.20), although in other works, such as his doctrinal treatise *On the Trinity*, Richard draws similitudes from
a consideration of the rational spirit's ability to love.

The fifth and final book of the *Mystical Ark* explores the
distinction between three *subjective modes* of appropriating
contemplation and their relation to grace and human effort.
"Enlargement of the mind" is a work of human effort in which
contemplation expands and sharpens the intellectual soul's
point of concentration, something that can take place by
acquiring an art, exercising it, and pursuing it with attention. This is the essential but not the sole mode found in the
stages of contemplation mediated by imagination and reason.
"Raising up of the mind" combines human effort and divine
grace on the level of contemplation mediated by the understanding. "Human understanding, when divinely inspired and

irradiated by that heavenly light, is raised up sometimes above knowledge, sometimes above activity, sometimes even above nature" (*Mystical Ark* 5.4). This takes place by means of divine revelation, that is, it is the realm of visionary experience. The primary concern of book 5, however, is with the third mode of experiencing contemplation, the "alienation of the mind." Although the *Mystical Ark* up to this point had primarily emphasized the intellectual side of progress to ecstatic contemplation, here Richard turns to the "flame of inner love" as described in the Song of Songs in order to understand the supreme forms of mystical experience found in this life. The Victorine shared the twelfth-century view that love and knowledge have reciprocal relations in the path to God, and that love (though an intellectualized love) has the dominant voice. "Surely the better we come to know the grace of perfection the more ardently we also desire it, and the more fully we are inflamed to love the more perfectly we are enlightened to recognition" (*Extermination of Evil and Promotion of Good* 2.9).

"Alienation of mind," according to Richard, is realized in three forms. The first is by "greatness of devotion," when the mind is so heated by the flame of love that it liquefies and rises like smoke to God. The second is "greatness of wonder," which happens when the intellectual soul is so irradiated by divine light like a flash of lightning that it loses all sense of itself in awe and wonder, driven down to the depths and then rising to the heights in its desire for God. Finally, "greatness of exultation" takes place when

... the human mind is alienated from itself, when having drunk of the inner abundance of interior sweetness,

indeed fully inebriated by it, the mind completely forgets
what it is and what it has been and is carried on into
an ecstasy of alienation by the excess of its dance and
is suddenly transformed into a form of supermundane
attraction under the influence of a state of wondrous
happiness. (*Mystical Ark* 5.5)

Richard finds biblical types for this form of contemplation
that takes the soul out of itself. The first is the Queen of
Sheba (3 Kings 10), who burned with love for Christ, the
true Solomon. She sought him out, plied him with questions, and finally, filled with awe at what she heard and
saw, fainted away in ecstasy. This describes the passage from
meditation, through contemplation, to alienation (5.12). The
second form, illustrated by the story of St. Peter's imprison-
ment and freeing by angelic intervention in Acts 12, typifies
how a devout soul, even in the midst of trial and temptation,
and before undertaking any effort of meditation, can be lifted
up to ecstasy by the grace of divine inspiration (5.13). The
final form of ecstasy described in 5.14–19 is the greatness of
exultation illustrated by the love of the Bride of the Song
of Songs herself. Richard's association of joy, exultation, and
even jubilation with the highest state of mystical experience
points to a new note of ecstatic rejoicing that was to find
increasing favor among the mystics of the later Middle Ages.

DYNAMICS OF LOVING

In his *Four Degrees of Violent Charity*, Richard's most personal
work, he examines the dynamics of loving, both love relationships between human lovers and the love between finite

subject and infinite subject. This work, marked by the Victorine's characteristic psychological insight, represents a new understanding of yearning love as self-transcending precisely because it is rooted in the absolute transcendence of the persons of the Trinity. The *Four Degrees* can best be seen as the mystical corollary of the doctrinal breakthrough Richard achieved in *On the Trinity*. The latter work sets out what we can know of the mystery of the infinite interpersonal love in the Trinity and thus provides the basis for understanding the violent, yet paradoxically also ordered, love with which a finite subject can express both its proper love for another finite subject and also the love it directs toward the three infinite subjects who are the Trinity.

The *Four Degrees of Violent Charity* takes as its major theme the interpretation of the book of the experience of love, conceived of as the most basic and most forceful of all human drives. With the book of experience as his primary text, reinforced by the Song of Songs, Richard founded his transformation of the language of love on the experiential dynamics of interpersonal relations. The violence and madness of love, especially of human erotic love, was no new discovery. The sickness attendant upon yearning desire was an important theme of the courtly literature that became popular in the twelfth century. If the charity that is the inner life of the Trinity is the ultimate source of all love, then it is also the archetype of the violence that is destructive when love is directed to the wrong goals, though consummating when love is rightly ordered.

Richard posits the highest form of love as "that burning and fervent love which penetrates the heart and enflames the affection and pierces the soul to the very marrow so that it

can truly say, 'I am wounded by charity' " (*Four Degrees* no. 2).
In his orderly scholastic way, Richard structures his treatise
with four stages of the violence of charity: "Behold, I see
some wounded, some bound, some languishing, some fainting
away, and all from charity. Charity wounds, charity binds,
charity languishes [i.e., makes ill], and charity brings on a
faint" (*Four Degrees* no. 4). This fourfold distinction pertains
to the violence of all loving, both sacred and profane — it
speaks the inner essence of love.

> *Richard's association of joy, exultation, and*
> *even jubilation with the highest state of mystical*
> *experience points to a new note of ecstatic*
> *rejoicing that was to find increasing favor among*
> *the mystics of the later Middle Ages.*

The psychological state induced by each of the four levels
is the same whether it is realized in sacred or profane love; the
effect on the loving subject, however, will be quite different.
Wounding love pierces the soul so that it burns with feverish
desire for the beloved. Binding love captures the lover in a
state of constant preoccupation with thoughts of the beloved.
Languishing love is a state of tyranny in which the love that
is experienced excludes everything else. Finally, the love that
causes one to faint away or die is a state of permanent desire
in which the burning soul can find no satisfaction. "It always
finds something still to desire.... It thirsts and drinks, but its
drinking does not extinguish its thirst" (*Four Degrees* no. 14).
  In the psychological progression of the madness of love
these four levels have very different effects, depending on

the person to whom they are directed. "In spiritual desires the greater the degree of desire the better; in fleshly desires the greater the worse" (*Four Degrees* no. 18). The reason for this is not so much Richard's undervaluing of human love or sexual desire, however much he may have shared medieval Christian ambivalences about these, but rather the analysis of finite and infinite love objects discussed in *On the Trinity*. The dynamic drive of the love planted in the human subject is our participation in the infinite love of the divine persons. Its insatiable character is our share in this infinity. When this insatiability is directed to the Divine Lover it allows a growth and ordering of love that benefits the human lover as well as all humanity; but when it is mistakenly directed to another finite person, love becomes perverted and its insatiability, unable to feed on the only truly infinite subject, eventually destroys both the lover and the human beloved.

For Richard, only the first level, wounding love (also called insuperable love), is healthy in human love relations. He identifies this with the highest form of human love, that which binds two people in marriage. The other forms of love, when directed to finite lovers, become increasingly destructive. Binding love, also called inseparable love, prevents us from fulfilling our responsibilities to other loves; languishing love, or singular love, frustrates the lover, who cannot enjoy the beloved as much as he or she would wish, while insatiable love can actually destroy both lover and beloved. When the violence of love is directed to the Divine Lover in the ascent to contemplation, however, love's logic reverses itself — the higher and more insane the love, the more satisfying and creative it becomes.

Richard illustrates the progression of sacred *eros* by a series
of images and illustrations drawn from the Bible and from
human marriage considered as a progression from betrothal,
through the marriage ceremony, sexual consummation, and
finally the bearing of children. In the betrothal stage, the
human lover deserts the world and turns away from carnal
pleasure through the influence of a grace that enflames the
affections but does not yet illumine the intellect. The stage
represented by the marriage ceremony is one of illumination
in which the soul flies up on the wing of contemplation to
a knowledge of heavenly mysteries. The most directly erotic
level is that symbolized by human sexual union, the stage
in which the mind is ecstatically united with the Divine
Bridegroom by being "rapt into the abyss of divine light."

This, however, is not the end of the process. Along with
all the major Christian mystics, Richard insists that mystical
experience is not just for the self but for the whole human
community. Sexual congress leads to childbirth, that is, the
soul passes through the ecstasy of mystical death in order
to be reborn with Christ and to continue his saving work
of love in the world. Such a soul abandons the delights of
mystical marriage to return to the active love symbolized by
the duties of a busy mother. "Doesn't this grade of love seem
to turn the intellectual soul mad since it does not allow it to
keep to mode or measure in its passion?" he asks. "Doesn't it
seem the height of madness to reject true life, to bring a case
against the highest wisdom, to resist omnipotence? Didn't he
reject life who was willing to be separated from Christ for his
brethren?" (*Four Degrees* no. 46).

This is the true insanity of loving God. Just as the fundamental law of the Christian life is that one can gain one's

life only by losing it (Matt. 10:39), so too the true ordering of charity involves the insanity of love that drives the mystic to abandon even the experience of divine love itself, imitating the love by which the Divine Lover emptied himself to bring his saving love to humanity. Richard of St. Victor's evocation of this essential truth aptly summarizes the contributions of twelfth-century mystics to the great tradition that God is never sought for ourselves alone, but always for the building up of the Body of Christ.

CONCLUSION

How did Richard learn so much about the motions of the human heart? If he was not one who entered into the highest levels of contemplation, how did he know so much about the experience? We do not have any personal testimony from him to help us answer these questions, but we know he was an educated man, aware of the themes and currents of his time, including the themes of courtly love. Richard was involved in the throbbing cultural and intellectual life of Paris; a teacher, a confessor, a religious, perhaps a spiritual director, and an administrator of a major center of learning. So we are left to speculate that he absorbed, with a finely tuned mind and heart, all that his culture, his tradition, and his personal relationships could teach him. To us he has left the result: a beautifully ordered study of how the human heart develops its innate capacity to love, how the human mind develops its capacity to understand, and, with intense effort and the gift of divine grace, how the human soul can reach far beyond itself to enter into the measureless abyss of interpersonal love that is the Trinity.

SUGGESTIONS FOR FURTHER READING

The best anthology of Richard's mystical writings is Richard
of St. Victor, *The Twelve Patriarchs; The Mystical Ark; Book
Three of the Trinity*, translated by Grover A. Zinn, Classics of
Western Spirituality (New York: Paulist Press, 1979). In addition, Richard's important treatise, the *Four Degrees of Violent
Charity*, is available in Richard of Saint-Victor, *Selected Writings on Contemplation*, translated by Clare Kirchberger (New
York: Harper & Brothers, n.d.). On Richard's mysticism, see
Steven Chase, *Angelic Wisdom: The Cherubim and the Grace
of Contemplation in Richard of St. Victor* (Notre Dame, Ind.:
University of Notre Dame Press, 1995). A general introduction to the Victorines and the world of early scholasticism
can be found in M.-D. Chenu, *Nature, Man, and Society in
the Twelfth Century: Essays on New Theological Perspectives in
the Latin West* (Chicago: University of Chicago Press, 1968).

Part Two

TRANSFORMATION IN GOD

Seven

Endless Pursuit

GREGORY OF NYSSA

LIFE AND WRITINGS

Gregory, born about 335, was the younger brother of the illustrious Basil; both were sons of an aristocratic family of Cappadocia in Asia Minor. Basil received the best possible education in rhetoric and philosophy, and Gregory appears to have been educated at home, probably under Basil's influence. Though he never cites sources, in his wide acquaintance with ancient philosophy Gregory was second to none among the great teachers of orthodox Christianity of his time. According to Gregory, it was their sister Macrina

who convinced Basil to abandon a secular life and be baptized in 356. The forceful Basil adopted the monastic way of
life and became a leader of what has been called "the ascetic
takeover" of Christianity. Gregory admired the monastic life,
but he himself was married — the only one of our twelve
mystical writers to be so.

After Basil was ordained priest in 364 and then made
bishop of Caesarea in 370, he turned to public action,
becoming the leader of the fight against those (Arians and
Semi-Arians) who refused to accept the Council of Nicaea's
declaration that the Son was consubstantial and therefore
fully equal to the Father in divinity. Basil corralled his
school-chum Gregory of Nazianzen and his younger brother,
Gregory, into accepting episcopal sees to aid him in this
struggle, though neither had much love or skill for politics.
It was through their writings against the Arians that the
two Gregorys came to be numbered with Basil as the "Cappadocian Fathers." Although Gregory of Nyssa was present
at the Council of Constantinople in 381, which reaffirmed
the teaching of Nicaea, and despite the fact he was a noted
preacher, his career after Basil's death, that is, from 379 down
to his own demise in 394, was largely devoted to his reading,
writing, and preaching. During these years Gregory composed important doctrinal and exegetical works, as well as
a deathbed dialogue with Macrina, *On the Soul and Resurrection*, a Christian adaptation of Plato's account of the death
of Socrates. Several of the bishop's writings can be described
as mystical in the sense that they center on how the devout
Christian should pursue a life of asceticism, prayer, and virtuous practice that aims at a direct perception of God in this
life. Among these writings are the treatises *On Virginity* and

On the Beatitudes, and two masterworks, the Life of Moses, an allegorical exposition of the life of the patriarch as a model for the God-seeking soul, and the fifteen Homilies on the Song of Songs, which Gregory sent to the Christian widow Olympias perhaps around 390.

FUNDAMENTALS OF
GREGORY'S THEOLOGY

Like most patristic authors, Gregory never wrote a systematic exposition of his theology; his works are polemical, exegetical, and occasional. Nevertheless, the Cappadocian sought to discern the inner logic connecting the events recounted in scripture and their extrapolation in theological discourse. Given the originality of Gregory's thought, a brief look at the power and profundity of his theological vision will help situate his contribution to mysticism.

Like the Greek philosophers, especially Plato, Gregory taught that God must be identified with supreme being and goodness. In chapter 20 of his major dogmatic work, the Catechetical Oration, he says: "Everyone agrees that we must confess the divine to be not only powerful, but also just, good, and wise, and whatever leads the mind upwards to some noble idea." In the Life of Moses God reveals himself in the burning bush as "True Being," or the "Really Real" (Life 2.23–25, 154, 235). Where Gregory and the other Cappadocians broke with traditional philosophical views of the divine nature was in their insistence on God's infinity and consequent incomprehensibility. Because there can be no limit to the divine nature, God is essentially incomprehensible in Godself — not just because of the weakness of the human mind. God is not just beyond the mind; God is "above the beyond" (*Commentary on Ecclesiastes* 7).

Most ancient philosophers (Plotinus is a notable exception) equated infinity with imperfection. Whatever truly exists, even the highest existence, must have a form of some kind, and that implies a limit. Origen shared this view and used it to help explain the fall of the spirits from the first creation. According to the Alexandrian, the spirits reached "satiety" in their contemplation of God and hence, in the exercise of their freedom, were able to turn away. Eunomius, the foremost spokesman for the Arian cause at the time of Basil and Gregory, was a skilled logician who asserted that there could be clear knowledge of God as the unbegotten nature and that this necessarily excluded the Son from the sphere of divinity. The Cappadocians knew and used Origen's writings, but they decisively broke with him, as well as with Eunomius and the Arians, in their doctrine of God.

The second major area in which Gregory made notable contributions to doctrinal and speculative theology was in his teaching on the Trinity. Although the essence of God remains an unfathomable mystery, in the order, or economy, of creation and redemption, God is revealed as a Trinity of Father, Son, and Holy Spirit. The fundamental task of "theology" (that is, speech about God) is to work out the proper language about God as three and one that reflects the biblical teaching and the church's confession of faith. Following Basil, Gregory took up the term *hypostasis,* or person, to signify the triplicity of Father, Son, and Spirit, and *ousia* and *physis* (substance and nature) to indicate the divine unity. The decisive shift to a relational understanding of *hypostasis* was a key moment in the development of the Christian understanding of the Trinity. Henceforth, the formula "one substance and three persons" was to be the touchstone of orthodox belief.

Basil and Gregory rebutted Eunomius's theology by showing that the attribute unbegotten, or ingenerate, was not something descriptive of the divine substance and therefore a "common attribute," but was a distinctive property of the hypostasis of the Father. Gregory's brief treatise *To Ablabius, On Not Three Gods* is one of the earliest attempts at creating a logic of trinitarian language. In order to protect the unknowability of the divine nature, Gregory and Basil also initiated a doctrine that was to become standard in Eastern Orthodox theology, the distinction between the hidden divine essence and the divine energies manifested in the world. As Gregory puts it in the sixth of the homilies *On the Beatitudes:* "For he is invisible by nature, but becomes visible in his energies, for he may be contemplated in the things that are referred to him."

Among the fundamental ways in which we can contemplate God, according to Gregory, is from "the free decision of his Goodness" by which he created the world and humanity. The Cappadocian, like the other great fathers of the fourth and fifth centuries, broke with ancient philosophy by emphasizing God's creative freedom. God does not need the world, nor is God to be conceived of as the supreme force within the universal order of things. God is immanent within the universe that depends on him, but he is no less utterly transcendent and above it. Gregory sought to bring out the theological meaning of the account of creation found in Genesis in a number of important works, especially his *Commentary on the Hexaemeron* designed to complete (and in places to correct) what his brother had begun, and in his treatise *On the Making of Man* (ca. 380), one of the most profound patristic treatments of creation.

Gregory's view of creation is fundamentally anthropomorphic: humanity is the center and goal of the creative process. Like Origen, he conceives of freedom as the essential characteristic of human nature, the image of God mentioned in Genesis 1:26. Chapter 5 of the *Catechetical Oration* speaks of "the most excellent and precious of blessings, . . . the gift of liberty and free will. . . . What in every respect is made similar to the divine must certainly possess free will and liberty by nature." But Gregory corrected Origen's view of creation in important ways. Gregory has a dual view of creation, but it differs from that of Origen in denying the pre-existence of the soul and a prior fall. The Cappadocian interprets the firmament that divides the waters above from the waters below (Gen. 1:6–8) as signifying the first heaven that separates the intelligible world from the sensible world. Humanity is the only creature that exists in both worlds, being created as idea and perfect image and likeness of God in the intelligible world and also simultaneously created as Adam, or individual man, in the sensible world. This double creation is not a result of a prior sin, but is due to the Creator's foresight of Adam's fall through the misuse of freedom. Through the taking on of human nature by the Word, fallen humans can begin to exercise their freedom correctly, acquiring the virtues that will eventually lead back to the unification of all things with God (Gregory, like Origen, holds to a universal return; see *Catechetical Oration* 26). In the tradition of the Greek Fathers, Gregory sees the Incarnation primarily in terms of divinization. Speaking of the Word's coming forth from the bosom of the Father, he says: "It was not the impassibility of his nature that he changed into something that suffers, but, on the contrary he transformed our changeable and passible nature into impassibility, by means of its fellowship with what cannot change" (*Life of Moses* 1.30).

GREGORY'S MYSTICAL TEACHING

On the basis of this impressive theology the Cappadocian constructed an understanding of mysticism centered on the endless pursuit of the infinite God. As he put it in the first book of his treatise *Against Eunomius*: "Since the First Good is infinite in its nature, communion with it on the part of the one whose thirst is quenched by it will have to be infinite as well, capable of being enlarged forever." Gregory found the motif of infinite pursuit throughout scripture, but a key and oft-cited passage comes from Paul speaking of himself in Philippians 3:13 as "forgetting what lies behind but straining forward to what lies ahead." The negative, or apophatic, aspect of this *epektasis*, or "straining forward," was to have profound influence on Dionysius. Gregory, however, personalized his epektetic mysticism in a distinctive way. He accomplished this first of all by his exegetical analysis of the path to God in treating the life of Moses and the love story of the Divine Bridegroom and the soul portrayed in the Song of Songs. As in Origen, we are invited to mystical consciousness in and through the work of reading the Bible, inscribing the sacred text on the text of the soul. Second, Gregory's teaching on the spiritual senses and the different forms of what he called the "feeling of presence" (*aesthesis parousias*) gives his presentation of *epektasis* a dynamic yearning quality rarely equaled.

The Jewish philosopher-mystic Philo of Alexandria (d. ca. 50 C.E.) was the first to set forth Moses as the exemplar of mystical pursuit of God. His treatment had an impact on both Clement of Alexandria and Gregory. The Cappadocian's *Life of Moses,* however, was a new kind of text, a structured allegory of the mystical path that freely rearranged the biblical account to present a clear picture of Moses as the model of perfection in the virtues. "In the case of virtue," Gregory says, "we have learned from the Apostle [citing Phil. 3:13] that the one limit of perfection is the fact that it has no limit" (*Life,* Prologue 5). While the treatise is clearly a consideration of the progress in virtues necessary for the Christian life (whether written for monks, or more likely for priests), training in virtue is not merely moral in the modern sense, but has a necessarily mystical goal that involves an increasingly more intimate and satisfying perception of God that paradoxically is always the trigger for an increase in longing. In the *Life of Moses* 2.166 Gregory distinguishes between two parts of religious virtue — "that which pertains to the divine and that which pertains to right conduct, for purity of life is a part of religion." Virtue is thus the outward manifestation of inward transformation, as Gregory notes in the *Homilies on the Song of Songs* when he compares the virtues to shining lilies Christ places within the soul pictured as a crystal vase (*Hom.* 15.441–42).

Gregory's mysticism is characterized by a dialectic that strives to create a balance between knowledge and virtue, light and darkness, satisfaction and desire, seeing and not seeing. Due to its fundamentally exegetical expression, the

Cappadocian does not set out these dialectical duos in explicit fashion, but rather allows the biblical text to guide whichever side of the dialectic he wishes to stress in a particular context. Thus, while negation and darkness are dominant motifs in the *Life of Moses*, the *Homilies on the Song of Songs* offer more possibilities to explore mystical ascent as an increasing illumination of the soul. Like his contemporary Augustine, Gregory does not speak of mystical union (*hênosis*), though he does use terms indicating mingling, sharing, fellowship, and the like. His fundamental mode of language is the vocabulary of transformation and divinization. In the eighth Homily on the Song, for example, he says: "When the Word bids the soul that has advanced to approach him, it is immediately strengthened at his command and becomes what he wishes, that is, changed into something divine, and from the glory which the soul had, it is transformed into a loftier glory by a wonderful alteration" (*Hom.* 8.253–54). In commenting on Song of Songs 6:3, "I to my beloved and my beloved to me," Gregory says that when the soul can say this, she "confesses that her own beauty, the primal blessedness of our nature, has been transformed into Christ, made lovely in the image and likeness of the first and only True Beauty" [Gen. 1:26 and Rom. 8:29] (*Hom.* 15.439).

The Life of Moses

The *Life of Moses* is divided into two books: the first gives the biblical history (sections 16–77); the second (sections 78–318) presents the deeper contemplation of the meaning of the narrative. Gregory appears to be the first to read Exodus as a progressive series of three revelations about the divine nature. The first theophany was the sight of the burning bush (Exod. 3:1–15), an experience of illumination in which Moses comes to understand that God is the True Being in whom all other things participate (*Life* 2.19–41). This knowledge enables the recipient to see the partial truth, but also the limitations, of worldly philosophy. The second revelation is that of the theophany described in Exodus 20:18–21, where Moses approached God in the cloud atop Sinai (*Life of Moses* 2.152–69). This manifestation, which Gregory seems to restrict to leaders of the community as Moses was (2.158–60), involves darkness and unknowing. Gregory recognizes that this theophany seems to contradict the former, but he says that scripture teaches that the religious illumination of faith comes first, but "as the mind progresses and through an ever greater and more perfect diligence comes to apprehend reality, as it approaches more nearly to contemplation, it sees more clearly what of the divine nature is uncontemplated" (2.162). Sounding a note that will later be emphasized by Dionysius, Gregory continues: "This is the seeing that consists in not seeing, because that which is sought transcends all knowledge, being separated on all sides by incomprehensibility, as it were by some cloud" (2.163).

Gregory goes on to note that it was upon the mountain that Moses was shown the tabernacle not made with hands that is the celestial model for the tabernacle to be constructed on earth as the site of God's presence (Exod. 25:8–9). The Cappadocian's reading of this is significant for the Christological and ecclesiological aspect of his mysticism, a characteristic he shares with Augustine and most of the other mystics of the patristic period. The tabernacle not made with hands, as Paul taught (Heb. 9:11–12), is Christ, "the power and wisdom of God" (1 Cor. 1:24), who is both not made with hands in his divine nature, yet also made, or created, in taking on material composition (*Life* 2.174). But Christ's body, the lower tabernacle, is not only his human nature, but also his body that is the church, "since in many places the church is also called Christ by Paul" (*Life* 2.184).

"The soul must transform passion into passionlessness so that when every corporeal affection has been quenched, our mind may seethe with passion for the spirit alone and be warmed by the fire the Lord came to cast on earth."

— Gregory of Nyssa, *Homilies on the Songs of Songs*

The final theophany made to Moses as the model of mystical ascent is found in Exodus 33:7–23, the account of the patriarch's conversation with God in which he asks for a face-to-face vision of divine glory. God responds, "My face you cannot see, for no man sees me and lives" (33:19). Gregory, like many mystics, sought to resolve the contradiction between those scriptural texts that speak of seeing God and those prohibiting such vision. In his homily on the sixth Beatitude (Matt. 5:8: "Blessed are the pure of heart, for they shall see God") he places the essence of the vision in the soul's inner seeing of itself as the image of God: "If someone who is pure of heart sees himself, he sees in himself what he desires; and thus he becomes blessed, because when he looks at his own purity, he sees the archetype in the image." This notion that the desire and search itself is the actual seeing helps us understand the third theophany given to Moses. Although God forbids face-to-face vision, he places Moses in a "hollow in the rock," where God hides his glory by placing his hand over the opening, and then allows the patriarch a vision of his back. Gregory interprets this mysterious passage epektetically (*Life* 2.219–55) — we see God by following after him. The soul, Gregory says, of its own nature seeks to fly ever upward, "by its desire for heavenly things 'straining ahead for what is still to come'" (Phil. 3:13). The great Moses is one of the few who never put any limit to this upward movement" (2.227). Here the emphasis is not on cloud and negation, but on illumination and yearning desire for divine Beauty. Gregory says of Moses:

> He shone with glory. And although lifted up through such lofty experiences, he is still unsatisfied in his desire for more. He still thirsts for that with which he is filled to capacity, and he asks to attain as if he had never partaken, beseeching God to appear to him, not according to his capacity to partake, but according to God's true being. Such an experience seems to me to belong to the soul that loves what is beautiful. (2.230–31)

In this encounter Moses learns that God is absolutely unbounded (2.236–38). He also begins to appreciate the mystical paradox that constant movement into God is the same as being firmly stationed in the rock, that is, in the divine Goodness which is manifested most fully in Christ (2.243). "For, since Christ is understood by Paul as the rock (1 Cor. 10:4), all hope of good things is to be believed in Christ, in whom we have learned all the treasures of good things to be" (2.248). The goodness of virtue does not look the supreme Good in the face, but ever follows after it in *epektasis*.

The Homilies on the Song of Songs

The same message of constant pursuit of God is set forth in Gregory's homilies on the Song of love, though with different accents to fit the diversity of text. What is also significant about this other major mystical work of the bishop of Nyssa is how it sets forth his principles for the transforming reading of the Bible. Gregory certainly knew Origen's exegesis and reflects it in many particulars, but his own interpretation is based on the primacy of *epektasis*.

Gregory presents both a general defense of spiritual exegesis in the prologue to his commentary, as well as an analysis of the type of reading fitting the Song of Songs in the first half of Homily 1. In setting out the latter, he begins by emphasizing the necessity for transformation: "You who have put on Jesus Christ with his holy robe and been transformed with him into a state that is free from passion and more divine, listen to the mysteries of the Song of Songs" (*Hom.* 1.15). But how is one to attain this state of passionlessness so that the pure words of the Bridegroom and Bride are not dragged down to earthly, irrational passions? Here, Gregory turns to the Christian program of education (*paideia*) that Origen laid out in his commentary. Solomon, a figure for Christ, teaches us through three books. In Proverbs he acts like a father giving his young son rudimentary instruction; in the book of Ecclesiastes he adds higher teaching for the one who has learned to desire the virtuous life. The highest form of philosophy, however, is given in the Song of love:

> Solomon elevates above everything grasped by sense the
> loving movement of our soul towards invisible beauty.
> Having thus cleansed the heart in external things,

Solomon initiates the soul into the divine sanctuary by means of the Song of Songs. What is described there is a marriage; but what is understood is the mingling of the human soul with God. (*Hom.* 1.22)

This process of education involves three transformations. First comes the moral development that is the presupposition for a proper reading of the Song. Then there is a double gender reversal as the son of Proverbs becomes the Bride of the Song, and the feminine divine Wisdom becomes the male Bridegroom, the Incarnate Logos. Such forms of gender malleability are found in many later mystics. Gregory was one of the first to sense that in the encounter with God ordinary gender identities become fluid. The third transformation is even more paradoxical: the change of passionate human eros, which for Gregory is a mark of the fall, into "passionless passion for bodiless realities." Gregory describes it as follows:

The most acute physical pleasure (I mean erotic pleasure) is used mysteriously in the exposition of these teachings. It teaches us the need for the soul to reach out to the divine nature's invisible beauty and to love it as much as the body is inclined to love what is akin to it and like itself. The soul must transform passion into passionlessness so that when every corporeal affection has been quenched, our mind may seethe with passion for the spirit alone and be warmed by the fire the Lord came to cast on earth [Luke 12:49]. (*Hom.* 1.27)

Thus, in the Song of Songs Christ instructs the soul about inner purity by using words that seem to indicate the opposite, the sensual language of human eroticism. Gregory roots this unusual pedagogy in his teaching on *epektasis*. All "perception of the divine" is a paradoxical state in which enjoyment or pleasure is always simultaneously characterized by unceasing desire for further experience of God. Both the Bride of the Song and Moses, the archetypal mystic, illustrate this law of the mystical life: "So it is with all others in whom the desire for God is deeply embedded: they never cease to desire, but every enjoyment of God they turn into the kindling of a still more intense desire" (*Hom.* 1.32).

> *The deep correlation that Gregory made between his teaching on divine infinity and the hunger for God he felt in his heart seems to be his own dynamic insight into the spiritual life, and it enables us to see why the retiring brother of the dominating Basil is today seen as one of the major early Christian mystics.*

Gregory followed Origen in reading the Song of Songs through the lens of the spiritual senses; all the images of the Song can be translated into a rich teaching about how the soul's inner organs of perception become more and more attuned to the presence of God. However, the Cappadocian put his own stamp on the doctrine of the spiritual senses once again by reading them in an epektetic mode. For example, in interpreting the wound of love of Song 2:5 ("I am wounded with love"), Gregory initially follows Origen in joining the Song's wound with the image of Christ as the chosen arrow of Isaiah 49:2. But he then proceeds to draw out the trinitarian and epektetic character of the message in a distinctive way. God the Father, who is Absolute Love, sends the arrow, his Only-Begotten Son, whose triple point (faith, hope, and charity) has been dipped in the Holy Spirit, into the heart of the believer. When the Divine Arrow enters her heart, the Bride breaks out in praise of the wonderful wound. The imagery by which the action of the right and left hands of the Father as Archer send love into the heart joins with the nuptial imagery of Song of Songs 2:6, "His left hand is under my head and his right hand shall embrace me." God is both Archer and Bridegroom, and when love enters into the soul, she herself also becomes an arrow directed back to God by the divine love within her. Because God is both the source of our flight to him and the goal toward which we fly, the Bride exclaims, "Simultaneously I am carried away by his act of shooting and I am at rest in the hands of the Archer" (*Hom.* 4.129). The essence of this unusual picture is *epektasis:* the loving soul is always both at rest in her enjoyment of God's presence and yet flying forward toward the ineffable goal that continues to elude her.

CONCLUSION

We look in vain for evidence that being married influenced the teachings of Gregory of Nyssa in any way — neither to give him special insights nor to inhibit the profundity of his writing. His teaching on the paradoxical fusion of attainment and yearning gives his reading of the Song of Songs a flavor not found in Origen, both a greater erotic tension and a more systematic treatment of the mystery of how every perception of God is also felt as absence and stimulus to further search. The deep correlation that the Cappadocian made between his teaching on divine infinity and the hunger for God he felt in his heart seems to be his own dynamic insight into the spiritual life, and it enables us to see why the retiring brother of the dominating Basil is today seen as one of the principal early Christian mystics.

SUGGESTIONS FOR FURTHER READING

Gregory's two major mystical works are available in English. See Gregory of Nyssa, *The Life of Moses*, translated by Abraham J. Malherbe and Everett Ferguson, Classics of Western Spirituality (New York: Paulist Press, 1978); and Gregory of Nyssa, *Commentary on the Song of Songs*, translated by Casimir McCambley (Brookline, Mass.: Hellenic College Press, 1987). Other works of Gregory are St. Gregory of Nyssa, *The Lord's Prayer; The Beatitudes*, translated by Hilda C. Graef, Ancient Christian Writers 18 (New York: Paulist Press, 1954); and Saint Gregory of Nyssa, *Ascetical Works*, translated by Virginia Woods Callahan, Fathers of the Church 58 (Washington, D.C.: Catholic University Press, 1967). A recent introduction to Gregory and anthology of his writings is that of Anthony Meredith, *Gregory of Nyssa* (New York: Routledge, 1999). Also useful are *From Glory to Glory: Texts from Gregory of Nyssa's Mystical Writings*, edited by Jean Daniélou and Herbert Musirillo (New York: Scribner's, 1961); Ronald E. Heine, *Perfection in the Virtuous Life: A Study in the Relationship between Edification and Polemical Theology in Gregory of Nyssa's "De Vita Moysis"* (Cambridge, Mass.: Philadelphia Patristic Foundation, 1975); and Hans Urs von Balthasar, *Presence and Thought: An Essay on the Religious Philosophy of Gregory of Nyssa* (San Francisco: Ignatius Press, 1995).

Eight

The Body of Christ

AUGUSTINE OF HIPPO

LIFE

Augustine was born in 354, the child of a pious Christian mother, Monica, and a pagan father. A clever youth, Augustine found education the key to a wider world. By the age of nineteen, his reading of philosophy had turned him away from the wildness of his early teens, but for more than a decade he experimented with different religious options and lived with a young woman. While a teacher of rhetoric in Milan in the 380s, the pull of divine love so tellingly described in his

Confessions enabled him to do what the weakness of his fallen will could not — make a decisive commitment to Christ that involved not only baptism but also the choice of a celibate life typical of emerging Christian ideals of perfection.

Augustine returned to Africa in 391, where he founded a monastic community and was ordained priest. In 395, he was made bishop of Hippo, a small coastal town, where he spent the remaining thirty-five years of his life caring for his flock and engaged in a series of doctrinal disputes that shaped later Western theology. He began by writing against the Manichaeans (a sect he once belonged to), showing the fundamental goodness of creation. (Manichaeans taught that there were two creators: an evil god who was the source of material reality, and a good god who created the spiritual world.) During his entire career as bishop, he combated the Donatists, a North African sect that believed that the church was the assembly of the perfect and that the efficacy of the sacraments depended on the holiness of the minister. From 411 on, he was increasingly occupied with Pelagius and his followers, whose view of fallen humanity's ability to avoid sin he found deeply erroneous. Between 413 and 425, he wrote his famous *City of God,* a vast theology of history and an attack on the classical view of humanity and society. Augustine died in 430 with the barbarians besieging Hippo: an emblem of the decline of the ancient Roman Empire.

MYSTICISM IN AUGUSTINE'S EARLY WRITINGS

The bishop of Hippo did more than any other figure to shape the religious world of the West for more than a millennium. Disputes over Augustine's teaching extend down to the present, though they are not as severe today as they were in the sixteenth century, when both Catholics and Protestants claimed Augustine's patronage for their contending theological views. Debates about what Augustine meant touch many aspects of theology, not least of all mysticism. During the twentieth century a number of scholars doubted whether Augustine should be called a mystic, largely because he did not speak about the soul's union with God, but restricted union language to the bond that all Christians have in Christ as constituting his Body, that is, the church. But this is precisely why Augustine can be called "the Father of Christian Mysticism" (the phrase of John Burnaby): he roots the possibility for all Christians to experience a deep and transforming awareness of God's immediate presence in their participation in the corporate life of the church. It is only in and through Christ's Body that we can reach or attain God in this life and in the next.

Augustine's best-known work, the *Confessions*, written about 397, artfully demonstrates the central role of Christ and the church in his own movement toward God. The first three books show the sinful young Augustine moving further and further away from God, the only source of the happiness and love he so desperately seeks in created things. God's grace, however, turns him around and, through a series of intermediaries and incidents, gradually leads him back toward the Truth. In book 7 Augustine describes what could be called some initial mystical experiences he had at Milan in 386 under the influence of reading Plotinus and "other books of the Platonists." Augustine's descriptions of these events follow a three-stage pattern based on Plotinus: the first stage is an initial withdrawal from the sense world; the second is an interior movement into the depths of the soul; finally, there is a movement above the soul to a vision of God. As one passage puts it:

> And so, admonished to return to myself, I entered into my inmost parts with You leading me on. I was able to do this because You had become my helper. I entered and saw with my soul's eye (such as it was) an unchanging Light above that same soul's eye, above my mind.... He who knows truth knows that Light. Love knows it. O Eternal Truth and True Love and Beloved Eternity. (*Conf.* 7.10).

Augustine, however, found these initial glimpses of the Divine Light frustrating. He realized that although the Platonic philosophers had glimpsed the eternal birth of the Word from the Father, they had no knowledge of the Word's taking flesh and dying for our sins. Hence, he decisively parts company with Plotinus and the pagan philosophers in his insistence that he could not really gain the strength for a saving experience of God until he had accepted the Incarnate Christ as the mediator between God and humanity (*Conf.* 7.18–19). The Christological and by implication ecclesiological nature of Augustine's mysticism is already present, and it becomes more evident in the famous account of the experience at Ostia that Augustine and his mother enjoyed after his baptism and before his return to Africa (*Conf.* 9.10).

It is significant that this is a shared experience. All through the *Confessions* Augustine emphasizes that no one is damned alone and no one is saved alone. Our fallen nature comes to us from Adam, and sinfulness is always compounded in our

solidarity with others; it is through Christ and our participation in his Body that a more true, but still partial, experience
of God can be attained in this life. In comparison with the
Milan account, the Ostia experience is presented in language
that is more social in context, more affective in rhetoric, and
more complex in its appeal to transformed interior sensation.
"Raising ourselves up by a more burning affection to the 'Self-
Same' [i.e., God] ... ," he says, "we touched him slightly with
the entire stroke of the heart ... " (9.10).

As Augustine was writing these events down ten years
later, he meditated on the continuing presence of such brief
moments of closeness to God in book 10 of the *Confessions*.
The search for God "in the fields and broad precincts of memory" leads memory beyond itself "in the desire to touch You
where You can be touched, to cleave to You where such cleaving is possible" (10.17). True happiness is found in rejoicing
in God who is the Truth itself, the God who is paradoxically both *within* memory insofar as all consciousness of truth
is found in the mind, and yet *above* memory as its Creator
(10.24–26). This analysis culminates in one of Augustine's
most noted exclamations: "Late have I loved You, Beauty so
old and so new." Though he recognizes how far he still is
from God, at the end of book 10 Bishop Augustine testifies
to the vital role of the ongoing moments of mystical consciousness God grants him: "At times You introduce me from
within into a wholly unaccustomed state of feeling, a kind of
sweetness which, were it made perfect in me, would be not of
this world, not of this life. But my wretched weights cause me
to fall back and I am swallowed up in the usual run of things.
I am held fast; heavily weeping, but heavily held" (10.40).

MYSTICISM IN THE LATER AUGUSTINE

In his later life Augustine rarely speaks about his own experiences of God. As teacher and preacher, it was far more
important for him to guide his congregation and readers in
the proper understanding of the possibility of finding God
through the biblical message as taught by the church. The
bishop's *Homilies on the Psalms* (his longest work), as well
as his *Homilies on the Gospel and Epistles of John* and some
other texts, are the primary witnesses to his mature mystical
teaching. In these texts we hear the voice of the preacher
speaking to the whole Christian community, not to some
spiritual elite. Augustine, like the other fathers, believed that
every baptized person was called to deeper experience of God.
A look at three of the sermons he preached on the Psalms will
demonstrate his deeply ecclesial understanding of mysticism.

Augustine's presentation of Psalm 26:4–5 centers on what
it means "to contemplate the Lord's delight." Though he uses
the passage primarily to stress that full contemplation will be
found only in heaven, this sermon already contains many
of his central ideas about the relation of contemplation in
this life to the coming heavenly reward. Augustine emphasizes the intimate connection between the *domus Dei*, that
is, the heavenly home in which there will be "contemplation
of the Good that is unchanging, eternal, always remaining
the same," and the *templum Domini*, that is, the Body of the
church that Christ forms out of all the faithful and in which
he is present as the inner sanctuary. For this reason, the
Christian can say, along with the Psalmist, "I will become his
temple and will be protected by him." According to Augustine, even though I do not yet experience pure contemplation

or delight in the Absolute Good that is God, I can share in it in this world through my union with Christ the Head. "He said that he is in us here below, and therefore we are in him there above. . . . What a pledge we have that we are now eternally in heaven with our Head by faith, hope, and love, because he is with us on earth until the end of the world" (*Hom. on Ps.* 26.2.11).

"No one should be so contemplative that in his contemplation he does not think of his neighbor's needs; no one so active that he does not seek the contemplation of God."

— Augustine, *City of God*

This first text from the *Homilies on the Psalms* leaves open the question of whether or not there is any direct consciousness of the presence of God in this life by suggesting that this issue is less important than emphasizing the deep union with God that all Christians possess in the Body of Christ. Other sermons, however, begin from our union with Christ in his Body to explore the kind of consciousness of God's presence that believers should aspire to in this life.

Augustine's Homily on Psalm 41, preached between 410 and 414, is one of his most famous mystical texts. Augustine again insists that all progress to consciousness of God's immediate presence can take place only within the church, but he here expresses this in the language of personal desire reminiscent of the *Confessions* and suggested by the opening verse of the psalm, "As the deer desires fountains of water, so does my soul desire You, O God." The burning thirst that the

soul experiences is a desire for the illumination of the interior
eye by God's light — Augustine intertwines the language of
love and knowledge as he introduces his theme. The bishop's
allegorical explanation of the deer enables him to make two
points about our preparation for interior illumination: first, it
demands the destruction of our vices and imperfections; and
second, it needs the mutual support found in the Christian
community.

In the second part of the sermon Augustine turns to what
kind of vision is possible here below for the faithful soul. "I
have sought my God in order not only to believe, but also,
if possible, to see something of him." Following the model
of three stages of ascent found in the *Confessions*, Augustine
insists that God is not to be found in the things of this world,
however beautiful they may be, nor is he discovered in the
interior vision the soul has of itself and of incorporeal realities
such as justice. In order to "touch God," one cannot remain
in oneself, but one must pass beyond the self in ecstasy, as
verse 5 of Psalm 41 says ("I meditated on these things and
poured out my soul above myself"). This ecstasy is described
as the passage from the tabernacle of the church here on
earth to the heavenly *domus Dei*. The ascent is possible only
through the agency of the church. Augustine argues that it
is by meditating on the virtues of the saints, "the members of
the tabernacle," that the ecstatic transition comes about. To
give his own words:

> Ascending the tabernacle, the soul comes to the house
> of God. While it admires the members of the tabernacle
> it is thus led to the house of God by following a certain
> sweetness, an indescribable interior hidden pleasure. It

is as if a musical instrument sweetly sounded from the house of God, and while walking in the tabernacle he heard the interior sound and, led by its sweetness, he followed what had sounded, separating himself from every clamor of flesh and blood until he arrived at the house of God. (*Hom. on Ps.* 41.9)

The enjoyment of the "presence of the face of God" that Augustine describes here primarily in auditory metaphors can only be brief in this life. "With the fine point of the mind," he says, "we are able to gaze upon something unchangeable, though hastily and in part."

A passage from Augustine's Homily on Psalm 99, preached in 412, has the same ecclesial message, but adds corollaries in three areas: divine incomprehensibility; God's omnipresence; and the role of love in restoring the likeness to God that makes contemplative vision possible. The bishop begins by investigating what the second verse of the psalm means by saying, "Let all the earth give jubilation to the Lord." The whole of creation does give evidence of God, but in itself it does not provide the knowledge to speak about him. In order to discuss God rightly we must be able to think of him correctly, and in order to think of him we must draw near to him. Such direct contact of spiritual seeing of God requires the attention of the heart, the cleansed heart that we read of in Matthew 5:8 ("Blessed are the pure of heart for they shall see God"). But how is sinful humanity to attain the clean heart needed to see God?

The first part of Augustine's answer to this question concerns the moral purification already discussed in the sermon on Psalm 41. The bishop now stresses the inner significance

of this cleansing as the restoration of "the interior person created to the image of God" through progress in love (*caritas*),
especially the love of all our fellow humans. "You will draw
near to the likeness [of God] by the measure you advance
in love, and to the same degree you will begin to perceive
God" (*Hom. on Ps.* 99.5). What does it mean to perceive
God (*sentire Deum*)? It is not that God comes to us as if he
had been absent, or even that we actually go to him. God
is always present to us and to all things. It is we, like blind
persons, who do not have the eyes to see him — "The one
you wish to see is not far from you." We need to become like
God in goodness and loving thought in order to perceive him.
Such experiential contact will produce the higher knowledge
when we grasp that we can really say nothing that is worthy
of him. This is how Augustine puts his own form of negative
mysticism:

> When, as someone who is like him, you begin to draw
> near and to become fully conscious of God, you will
> experience what to say and what not to say, insofar
> as love grows in you, because "God is love" (1 John
> 4:18). Before you had the experience, you used to think
> that you could speak of God. You begin to have the
> experience, and there you experience that you cannot
> say what you experience. (*Hom. on Ps.* 99.6)

AUGUSTINE ON LOVE

The emphasis on the love of *caritas* is one of the central concerns of Augustine's mysticism. Throughout his life Augustine
remained a great lover, and his reflections on the role of love

in the path to God, as well as the relation of love and knowledge, are profound. According to the bishop, love is the soul's
weight — *pondus meum amor meus* (*Conf.* 13.9). By means of
the gift of divine love of *caritas* we have the power to ascend
to God, while through the self-centered love of *cupiditas* we
flee from him. For Augustine, "Each person is what he loves"
(*Homily on 1 John* 2.14). But the bishop knows that love and
desire presuppose some kind of knowing: we cannot love what
we are totally ignorant of. Where does such knowledge come
from in the case of God, who is by definition unknowable?

Faith, hope, and love are the key. In commenting on
verse 4 of Psalm 104 ("Seek his face always"), the bishop
provides a good short answer to the problem. To be always
seeking the face (i.e., the presence) of God seems to preclude
ever really finding him. But what the verse really means is
that God has already been found in faith, but still needs to
be ever sought after by hope while we are in this life. It is
love, the *caritas* that the Holy Spirit pours out in our hearts
(Rom. 5:5), which unites faith and hope. "Love both finds
him through faith and seeks to possess him through appearance where he is then found in such a way that he satisfies
us and is sought no longer" (*Hom. on Ps.* 104.3). The love
with which God first loved us (1 John 4:14) enters into our
hearts and gives us a new, if still obscure, knowledge of God
in faith. It also provides us with a new impetus of desire;
no longer the natural desire for God implanted in us at creation, but a longing for God that functions as a new eye
of the soul, the source of the ray of light that always pur-
sues the ineffable God. This new way of seeing is in us, but
not of us; it requires our cooperation, but its operation is
from God.

In commenting on Psalm 17, Augustine once again empha-sized the priority of love over knowledge, saying that God "rode far above the fullness of knowledge to show that no one could approach him save by love" (*Hom. on Ps.* 17.11). Therefore, the heart must first be healed before God can be seen or in some way known. This healing is the work of the Holy Spirit, who is Love itself, and it is carried on in the Body of Christ. The measure of our love is the measure of the vision that we can have of God, even in this life. "The more ardently we love God, the more certainly and calmly do we see him, because we see in God the unchanging form of justice, according to which we judge how one ought to live" (*On the Trinity* 8.19). For Augustine there is only one test for the authenticity of the love that we have for God — love of our neighbor. In his later works, such as the pro-found treatise *On the Trinity*, Augustine even insists that love of neighbor *is the same as* love of God. He explains: "This is because one who loves his neighbor must necessarily first have love for Love itself. But 'God is Love, and he who abides in Love, abides in God'" (*On the Trinity* 8.7). Such love leads to the fullness of knowledge, though we can experience this only in a partial way in this life, even in the brief flashes of ecstatic consciousness that God sometimes gives to those who ardently desire him.

OTHER ASPECTS OF
AUGUSTINE'S MYSTICISM

Love in the general sense (*amor*) is the glue by which we adhere to whatever we truly desire, and the love of charity is the higher glue that binds us to God. Augustine, as noted above, spoke of union with God in terms of the bond that knits all believers into the one Body of Christ. He does not discuss the union of the individual soul with God, but prefers instead to use a complex language of contact and interior perception based on the spiritual senses. Given his knowledge of Neoplatonic philosophers like Plotinus, who did speak of union with the One, it seems likely that the bishop's avoidance of union language was a deliberate critique of a form of mysticism that, for all its nobility, confused the difference between God and human and failed to recognize that what brings us to God is the divine gift of love given to us in the Body of Christ.

While Augustine did not talk about personal union with God, he did have much to say on what it means to "see God," as we have seen from the passages discussed above in book 7 of the *Confessions*. Letter 147, a treatise he wrote to the noblewoman Paulina in 413, analyzed at length what it means to see God. Augustine's accounts of immediate experiences of God, however, do not depend on the metaphor of vision alone. Rather, his combining of the language of seeing with metaphors drawn from the other spiritual senses constitutes a deliberate mixing, even a confusion, designed to convey something of the obscurity and ineffability of all close encounters with God. Tactile images are widely found in his writings, not only the language of touching, but especially that of clinging and cleaving to, embracing and sticking to, as suggested in a favorite Psalm text: "It is good for me to cleave to the Lord" (Ps. 72:28).

Another theme that underlines the altered forms of consciousness found in mystical contact with God is that of "spiritual drunkenness," developed from such texts as Psalm

35:9: "They will be inebriated by the richness of your house." Concerning the difficulty of speaking about such experiences, Augustine says: "My brethren, I dare say that in the matter of the holy words and movements of the heart through which the Truth is proclaimed to us we can neither say what they announce nor think it" (*Hom. on Ps.* 35.19). Augustine never thought that our immediate experiences of God in this life could be adequately expressed; they could only be hinted at through verbal strategies designed to suggest and not to circumscribe the mystery of God.

Augustine expended a good deal of thought on the relation between ordinary vision and the special forms of seeing by which God allows some glimpse of divine splendor. His thought is most fully laid out in the twelfth book of his *Literal Commentary on Genesis*. Augustine's theory of visions and ecstasy found here was to have a profound impact on later Western mysticism. The bishop's starting point is the puzzle over how to understand the visions of God ascribed to some key biblical figures, especially Moses and Paul. He approaches the issue by means of a distinction of three kinds of seeing, whether the objects of sight are presented to us by the created world, or by God's special action. Corporeal vision sees concrete objects, spiritual vision sees images in the mind, and intellectual vision is immediate understanding of truth without any image. The primary concern of book 12 is to explore how God can grant special objects of vision and the effect that this has on the recipient, namely, "ecstasy" (*ecstasis/excessus mentis*), terms that Augustine found in scripture. Ecstasy can sometimes be the product of natural causes, but Augustine is interested in the special acts of grace in which "the soul's intention is completely turned away or snatched away from the body's senses" (*Literal Commentary* 12.12). In these states the soul sees nothing by way of the senses; it is totally intent on imaginative or intellectual seeing within. God can grant both new images within the imagination, as we see in the case of the visions recounted in the Apocalypse, and he can also give direct intelligible awareness of divine truths. Regarding this highest, or intellectual, vision, Augustine says: "There the brightness of the Lord is seen, not through a symbolic or corporeal vision . . . nor through a spiritual vision, but through a direct vision and not through a dark image, as far as the human mind elevated by God's grace can receive it" (*Literal Commentary* 12.26).

Augustine claimed that a direct vision of God is possible in this life in moments of ecstasy. Scripture, he says, demonstrates this in the cases of Moses and Paul, though such miracles were not restricted to them. A text in the *Homilies on John* applies the highest form of vision to the evangelist as well, and the teaching found throughout the bishop's writings argues that he thought that the experience of the presence of Divine Truth in this life was something that all Christians were called to share in, though in ways and degrees known only to God. All such experiences, whether of spiritual or intellectual visions, however, are partial. Heaven alone is the land of "vision without defect and love without weariness," where "our whole task will be nothing but praising and enjoying God" (*Hom. on Ps.* 85.11 and 86.9).

The vision of God that can be attained in this life is possible only within God's tabernacle, that is, the church. Such vision involves the restoration of humanity's status as "image of God" (Gen. 1:26), something that had been deeply injured in Adam's fall. The restoration effected by grace reactivates the interior powers, the spiritual senses that were originally intended to lead us to God before their wounding by sin made this impossible. Through grace these powers can attain a direct, though temporary, experience of the presence of God, Father, Son, and Holy Spirit, something that is open to all Christians, at least potentially.

Augustine's insistence that true progress toward God must be thought of as social, that our pursuit of God is not a solitary effort, but one that takes place in the bosom of the church and by means of the exercise of loving charity toward all, is the core of his message.

Augustine's understanding of the universality of the call to mystical contact with God meant that he was resolutely opposed to the kinds of esotericism and elitism that argued that only select souls had the inner divinity that enabled them to attain God. The bishop's three sermons on John 16:12–13 (Jesus' promise of the coming of the Spirit of Truth) are a detailed investigation of the dangers of mystical esotericism. The "many things" that Christ still had to say to the disciples (John 16:12), truths to be made clear by the Spirit (16:13), are not esoteric secrets to be revealed after Christ's return to heaven. All true teaching comes from the Holy Spirit within us, not from merely human teachers. Therefore, the transition from the milk of simple teaching to an increasing diet of solid food spoken of by St. Paul (1 Cor. 3:2) is the work of Christ and his Spirit. Although Augustine admits that there will always be different levels of appropriation of the Christian message, the content is always one and the same, not divided into sections for different groups. Christ is received as milk by some and solid food by others, "because although they do not hear more, they understand more" (*Homily on John* 98.2). Hence, the bishop concludes, "there seems to be no necessity that some secret teachings are kept silent and hidden from the faithful who are still children in the manner of matters to be spoken privately to the advanced, that is, to the more intelligent" (*Hom.* 98.3). We are all equally members of the Body of Christ, though we function in different ways.

Christian mystics adopted and transformed the ancient Greek paradigm of the distinction between contemplation and action, as we have seen. What for the Greek philosophers had been a difference between two activities constituting two ways of life, the philosophical and the political, in the hands of Christian thinkers, beginning with Clement of Alexandria and Origen, had become a distinction between contemplation of God and the active charity to which Christians are called by the Gospel. While Christians agreed with Neoplatonic thinkers in shifting the meaning of contemplation away from discursive reasoning in the direction of suprarational awareness, they parted company with them in the Christian insistence that the contemplative life could never dispense with the active life. Augustine represents an important stage in this teaching and its transmission to later Western mysticism. Augustine summarizes his teaching on action and contemplation in the *City of God* when he comments on the three modes of life: contemplative, active, and mixed. In book 19 he says: "As long as faith is preserved, a person can lead any one of these lives and come to the eternal reward. What counts is how he holds to the love of truth and how he weighs the duties of charity. No one should be so contemplative that in his contemplation he does not think of his neighbor's needs; no one so active that he does not seek the contemplation of God." In other words, the Christian life must always be mixed, at least implicitly.

CONCLUSION

Augustine's influence on later mysticism was immense, although it was largely restricted to the Latin West. His views on the call to attaining direct and immediate consciousness of God in this life, as well as the solid Christocentric and ecclesial way in which he presented the mystical goal to the Christian community, were characteristic of many of the great mystics of the patristic period. His insistence that true progress toward God must be thought of as social, that our pursuit of God is not a solitary effort, but one that takes place in the bosom of the church and by means of the exercise of loving charity toward all, is the core of his message. The bishop's sense of the always fleeting and partial nature of our experiences of the presence of Christ and the Holy Spirit leading us back to the Eternal Father is found among many patristic writers, but it is rarely expressed with such power and in more compelling language. Augustine, as perhaps no other mystic, encourages us to engage in our own inner dialogue with God through meditation on our lives viewed in the light of the biblical message. He asks us to repeat along with him the immortal words: "You arouse a person to delight in praising You, because You have made us for Yourself, O God, and our heart is restless until it rests in You" (*Conf.* 1.1).

SUGGESTIONS FOR FURTHER READING

The literature on Augustine is vast, and a large number of his more than one hundred works have been translated. There are many versions of the *Confessions*. For an anthology of the bishop's spiritual writings, see *Augustine of Hippo: Selected Writings*, translated by Mary T. Clark, Classics of Western Spirituality (New York: Paulist Press, 1984). We are fortunate now to have a full and reliable translation of the first half (Psalms 1–72) of Augustine's magnificent homilies on the Psalms; see *Expositions of the Psalms*, translated by Maria Boulding, 3 vols., Works of St. Augustine: A Translation for the Twenty-first Century (Hyde Park, N.Y.: New City Press, 2000–2001). For a biography of Augustine and his times, Peter Brown, *Augustine of Hippo: A Biography* (Berkeley: University of California Press, 1967). For Augustine's mysticism, see such classic works as John Burnaby, *Amor Dei: A Study of the Religion of St. Augustine* (London: Hodder & Stoughton, 1938); Robert J. O'Connell, *St. Augustine's Early Theory of Man, A.D. 386–391* (Cambridge, Mass.: Harvard University Press, 1968); and Paul Henry, *The Path to Transcendence: From Philosophy to Mysticism in St. Augustine* (Philadelphia: Pickwick Press, 1981). For issues connected with Augustine, see also *Augustine through the Ages: An Encyclopedia*, Allan D. Fitzgerald, general editor (Grand Rapids: Eerdmans, 1999).

Nine

Unknowing Knowing

DIONYSIUS

LIFE

No one knows what his name really was. He wrote under the pseudonym Dionysius the Areopagite, St. Paul's Athenian convert (see Acts 17:34), and for centuries his writings were treated with quasi-apostolic authority. Martin Luther, among others, challenged this identity. Modern scholars put him in Syria, a monk writing around the year 500 C.E. Dionysius not only created the term "mystical theology," he also gave systematic expression to a dialectical view of the relation of God and the world that was the fountainhead of speculative mystical systems for at least a thousand years.

WRITINGS

The surviving writings that constitute the Dionysian corpus are four treatises and ten letters. The *Divine Names* (abbreviation *DN*), the central and longest surviving work, is made up of thirteen chapters dealing with the positive, or cataphatic, theology, describing conceptual terms or names of God as Creator. Cataphatic theology affirms divine attributes and qualities, such as "God is good; God is holy," etc. The *Divine Names* also introduces important elements of negative, or apophatic, theology. Apophatic theology emphasizes the fact that God is utterly unknowable and no human language can express anything true about the divine. Subsequent to the *Divine Names*, Dionysius apparently wrote an important treatise, *Symbolic Theology*, now lost, but referred to in his later works. Then he penned the brief but powerful work by which he is best known, the *Mystical Theology* (MT). He summarizes the relation between this treatise and the earlier works as follows:

> In my earlier books my argument traveled downward from the most exalted to the humblest categories.... But my argument now rises from what is below up to the transcendent, and the more it climbs, the more language falters, and when it has passed up and beyond the ascent, it will turn silent completely, since it will finally be at one with him who is indescribable. (MT 3)

This rising up into silence and unknowing in the face of the unknowable God is what Dionysius means by "anagogy." The lower stages of this upward way form the subject of the two remaining treatises. The *Ecclesiastical Hierarchy* (EH) treats of how the church's liturgy and offices function in the anagogic process. The *Celestial Hierarchy* (CH) investigates how the scriptural descriptions of the nine choirs of angels are to be understood as playing their part in our uplifting to God. The major treatises can be understood in terms of a triadic structure: *Divine Names* is primarily concerned with procession from the Source; *Ecclesiastical Hierarchy* and *Celestial Hierarchy* deal with lower stages of reversion to God, and *Mystical Theology* completes the account of reversion and concludes by saying what little can be said about God in himself through a series of supereminent expressions. In addition, ten letters ascribed to Dionysius survive, touching on various aspects of his mystical teaching.

DIONYSIUS'S THEOLOGICAL PROGRAM

In developing his theological program, Dionysius synthesized both the Christian and the Neoplatonic strands of thought to which he was heir. As a result, readers over the centuries have disagreed as to whether the Areopagite was more Christian or more Neoplatonic as a thinker. For Dionysius himself, this does not appear to have been a problem. His theological center of concern is the exploration of how the utterly unknowable God manifests himself in creation in order that all things may attain union with their one unmanifest Source. The task Dionysius took on himself was to portray the divine self-unfolding in an objective way. Since our only access to

the hidden God is by way of God manifested in creation, all
theology begins with the consideration of the God-world relation. While Dionysius recognized that Neoplatonic thinkers
provided useful resources for addressing these concerns, he
was certain that the only true resolution was to be found in
biblical revelation.

The Dionysian program is cosmic. Divine Eros refracts
itself into the multiple theophanies, or divine manifestations,
found in the universe, and these effects in turn erotically
strive to pass beyond their multiplicity back into the simple
unity that is the divine. The whole universe is characterized by being, goodness, and beauty: "Any thinking person
realizes that the appearances of beauty are the signs of invisible loveliness" (*CH* 1). Dionysius's dialectical view of the
relation of creation to the Creator revolves around the problem of how the unknown God always remains totally *identical*
with himself, while still *overflowing* into differentiation in his
effects (creation), in order eventually to regain identity by
reversion of all things back into himself. In weaving together
the themes of the pagan Neoplatonic authors with the Christian tradition, Dionysius saw the universe as a beautiful circle
of longing love. Creation originates in the divine Eros; the
overflowing of Goodness is multiplied into all the individual elements of creation. Each created unit participates in its
own share of eros, longing love for God, and desires to return
to be reunited with the divine Eros. The "Light beyond all
divinity," which is identical with the "Nameless Itself" (*DN*
1.6), "is at a total remove from every condition, movement,
life, imagination, conjecture, name, discourse, thought, conception, being, rest, dwelling, unity, limit, infinity, the totality
of existence" — that is, it always remains in itself. "And yet,

since it is the underpinning of goodness, and by merely being there is the cause of everything, to praise this divinely benefi-cent Providence you must turn to all of creation." This is the task of cataphatic theology. But the positive path demands the return to the negation founded on our need to go beyond all things to their supernal Source. Concerning this mystery, Dionysius says: "All things long for it. The intelligent and rational long for it by way of knowledge, the lower strata by way of perception, the remainder by means of stirrings of being alive." Apophatically, all things long to return to the source (*DN* 1.5).

> "My *argument now rises from what is below up to the transcendent, and the more it climbs, the more language falters, and when it has passed up and beyond the ascent, it will turn silent completely, since it will finally be at one with him who is indescribable.*"
>
> — Dionysius, *Mystical Theology*

Dionysius created two new terms in developing his teach-ings about the relation of God to creation. The first is "thearchy." This was his word for the triune God who com-municates himself in creation. The providence of thearchy reaches all things and "transcendentally draws everything into its perennial embrace" (*CH* 7.4). His other new term — one that caught on in the tradition, as thearchy did not — was "hierarchy." God as the triune thearchy, the Christian Trinity, is the principle or source of the universe, which is conceived of primarily as a hierarchy, that is, a multiple yet

ordered manifestation of the divine source. The powers of
purification, illumination, and perfection that make possible
the return to God are present in the hierarchies of the created
universe, because they are all participations in the thearchy.
In order to manifest the Trinity, every hierarchy must be both
one and three, and so every hierarchy will have three levels:
one that purifies, one that enlightens, and one that perfects.

Thus, every hierarchy will contain those who act, those
who mediate, and those who are acted upon. In the human
realm the ecclesiastical hierarchy functions with three orders
of sacred agents who use three rituals to divinize three groups
of Christians, because "the goal of a hierarchy . . . is to enable
beings to be as like as possible to God and to be at one
with him" (*CH* 3.2). The sacraments of baptism, Eucharist,
and anointing are performed by deacons, who purify; priests,
who illuminate; and bishops who perfect (*EH* 2–5). This is
done for the benefit of catechumens, who are being purified;
the baptized, who are being enlightened; and the monastics, who are being perfected (*EH* 6). Obviously, Dionysius
did not think that all Christians should become monks or
bishops. What is divinizing about the hierarchy is not where
one stands in it, but the understanding that comes as one
grasps the divine activity manifested in the interrelations of
the ordered whole. The workings of the celestial hierarchy of
the angels is similar. What is divinizing and anagogic for us
is the proper interpretation and understanding of the angels
as multiple manifestations of the divine beauty.

The Dionysian understanding of hierarchy also helps us to
understand his Christology. Dionysius speaks of Christ less
frequently than many other mystics, but this does not mean
that the Godman is unimportant for him. Dionysius shows

evidence of his personal devotion to Jesus the Christ in a number of places, including his prayer at the beginning of the *Celestial Hierarchy* that his work will be guided "by Christ, by my Christ" (CH 2.5). In *Ecclesiastical Hierarchy* 1.2 he calls on "Jesus, the source and perfection of every hierarchy," though the role Jesus plays in the hierarchies is not made very explicit here. There are texts, however, that demonstrate the role of Jesus in both the celestial and the ecclesiastical hierarchies. The highest hierarchy of angels is said to be contemplative because they have entered "into communion with Jesus . . . by truly coming close to him in a primary participation" (CH 7.2). Furthermore, the sacraments of baptism, Eucharist, and anointing all effect participation in Jesus and his saving work. Perhaps the most significant aspect of the Areopagite's teaching about Jesus' hierarchical activity is its motive force: love. Again and again he emphasizes the Incarnation as a work of divine love, and more tellingly he says that to affirm this truth is to begin to negate the world and thus return to God. "Every affirmation regarding Jesus' love for humanity has the force of a negation pointing towards transcendence" (Letter 4).

DIVINE GOODNESS AS UNIVERSAL EROS

Dionysius created a theory of Eros both cosmic and divine that was to be one of his most profound contributions to Christian theology. In the *Divine Names* the Areopagite starts out with the first and most important name for God, "Good." The self-giving nature of Goodness implies the power of Goodness to move all things toward it as a goal. Therefore, for Dionysius the Good and the Beautiful are identical. Further, in *Divine Names* 4 he sees Eros as both identical with

Good-Beauty and as the dynamic power by which thearchy expresses itself in hierarchy. If the Good has priority among the positive names of God, it is precisely because it is understood as Eros or divine "Yearning." "And we may be so bold," Dionysius continues, "as to claim also that the cause of all things loves all things in the superabundance of his goodness, that because of this goodness, he makes all things, brings all things to perfection, holds all things together, returns all things." Dionysius concludes with his definition of God as Eros: "Divine Eros is the Good of the Good for the sake of the Good" (*DN* 4.10). But Dionysius goes even further by insisting that divine Eros must be ecstatic, or outside itself:

> It must be said that the very cause of the universe in the beautiful, good superabundance of his benign yearning for all is carried out of himself in the loving care he has for everything. He is, as it were, beguiled by goodness, by love and by yearning and is enticed away from his dwelling place and comes to abide with all things, and he does so by virtue of his supernatural and ecstatic capacity to remain, nevertheless, within himself. (*DN* 4.13)

In other words, God alone can totally go out of himself in a complete ecstasy of self-giving because he alone has the ability to remain absolutely within himself, utterly transcendent to all things. He loves himself *in* all things from the very same ground and for the very same reason that he loves himself *beyond* all things.

Dionysius was the first to express this dialectical understanding of God primarily in terms of Eros. God is both the *object* of the yearning of all things to return to him and he is also that *very yearning itself* as participated in by all levels of the individual hierarchies. In the circle of love that forms the Dionysian universe we have a God who becomes ecstatic in procession and a universe whose ecstasy is realized in reversion back to God. God is the direct and immediate cause of all things as individuals and in all their particular qualities, so that all things are beautiful manifestations of the ecstatic divine Eros. Every individual thing is a created reflection of the divine mind. The most important truth about the cosmos is the direct relation of absolute dependence that each individual reality has to the thearchy that creates all things. From the human perspective, the understanding of the activities of the hierarchies reveals the immediacy of all creatures to divine Eros. This is the heart of Dionysius's distinctive Christian Neoplatonism.

DIONYSIUS'S THEORY OF MYSTICISM

Basic Assumptions

Dionysius never ascribes to himself a special experience of the divine presence, though he does appeal to the witness of those who had been granted such experiences: Moses and Paul, and his teachers Carpos and Hierotheus. To understand his map of the spiritual journey back to God, we must take note of some basic assumptions. First of all, Dionysius, adhering to the tradition of his Christian predecessors, emphasizes that the anagogic life of the believer is fundamentally ecclesial and liturgical. The uplifting process that returns us to union with God is one that is accomplished through the interaction of the three essential aspects of the life of the church: (1) the proper understanding of scripture; (2) in and through the action of the sacred liturgical rituals; (3) performed (or received) according to one's place in the ecclesiastical hierarchy. Evagrius had insisted, "If you are a theologian you truly pray," understanding prayer primarily as an individual contemplative exercise. Dionysius would claim that to be a true theologian is to pray liturgically. Both would agree that to be a true theologian one would have to be what later centuries would call a mystic.

A second basic assumption is the way Dionysius understands reversion, or anagogy, the process of uplifting and returning to God. Given his conception of the whole created hierarchy as an ordered manifestation of thearchy, Dionysius teaches that one does not really *ascend to* God by passing through various levels of reality; rather, one *appropriates the significance* of the levels as a means of attaining inner union with their source, the hidden God. The spiritual journey upward is really a journey inward to deeper understanding within the soul.

A third basic assumption involves the Areopagite's use of the term "mystical." It was he more than anyone who gave the word the importance it continues to enjoy in Christian thought. Dionysius is most noted for the creation of the concept "mystical theology," a technical term that refers not to a particular kind of experience but to the knowledge (or, better, "super knowledge") that deals with the mystery of God in himself. But the whole of Dionysius's thought is mystical, since the interaction of all the modes of theology has as its goal attaining union with God in darkness and silence. Did Dionysius ever use "mystical" in a more subjective or experiential way? In *Divine Names* 2.9, speaking of the doctrine that his teacher Hierotheus acquired either directly from the authors of scripture or from the study of their writings, he speaks of a third and higher type of knowledge in which Hierotheus " ... was initiated into them [i.e., divine truths] by some more divine inspiration, not only learning the things of God but experiencing them, and through this sympathy with them, if we may say this, having been consummated in initiation into mystical union and faith in them which cannot be taught." For Dionysius this personal "sympathy" is an affinity for "reading" the inner meaning of the hierarchies as manifestations of thearchy.

When we compare these passages on Hierotheus with those in which Dionysius treats his other exemplary mystics, Moses, Paul, and Carpos, we notice a pattern: the special experience, knowledge, and vision that these mystics received is described in language similar to that used in the *Ecclesiastical Hierarchy* for the celebration of the liturgy. So, if Dionysius can be said to include elements of a more existential dimension to the term "mystical" (though always ascribed to his teachers and not to himself), this experience is liturgical and ecclesial in setting and context. The *Mystical Theology* is inseparable from the *Ecclesiastical Hierarchy*. For example, Moses, as the ideal mystic, first undergoes purification, then gains contemplation of the place (not the essence) of God, and finally attains union. According to the *Mystical Theology*:

> Here, renouncing all that the mind may conceive, wrapped entirely in the intangible and the invisible, he belongs completely to him who is beyond everything. Here, being neither oneself nor someone else, one is supremely united by a completely unknowing

inactivity of all knowledge, and knows beyond the mind
by knowing nothing. (MT 1.3)

This triple pattern of purification, illumination, and perfection or union, which appeared earlier in Origen and Evagrius,
was to remain one of the most common ways to understand
the mystical itinerary. Dionysius's use of the pattern, however,
has to be viewed through his understanding of the operation
of different modes of theology in the life of the believer. As
he says:

Theological tradition has a dual aspect, the ineffable
and the mysterious on the one hand, the open and
more evident on the other.... The one resorts to symbolism and involves initiation. The other is philosophic
and employs the method of demonstration.... The one
uses persuasion and imposes the truthfulness of what
is asserted. The other acts and, by means of a mystery which cannot be taught, it puts souls firmly in the
presence of God. (Letter 9.1)

"Theological tradition" here means the total life of the
church in which Bible and liturgy are used both positively
to teach truths about God and negatively to make the divine
mystery present in ways that cannot be demonstrated. What
cannot be demonstrated can still be made present on the
material level of the symbols used by scripture and the liturgy and also on the intellectual level, where the negation
of names of the divine and eventually the removal of both
affirmation and negation bring the soul to union with the
divine mystery. For Dionysius, both affirmation and negation
are necessary, but negation always has priority by being more

directly related to the divine transcendence. Since "God is in no way like the things that have being and we have no knowledge at all of his incomprehensible and ineffable transcendence and invisibility" (CH 2.3), the way of negation is superior to that of affirmation.

All things, then, both reveal and conceal God. The "dissimilar similarity" that constitutes every created manifestation of God is both a similarity to be affirmed and a dissimilarity that denies anything is really like God. The universe is both necessary as an image and impossible as a representation of the God for whom there is no adequate representation. Nevertheless, it is only in and through immersion in the beauty of the universe that we can discover that God is always more than we can conceive. Likewise, on the symbolic level we find God in the positive symbols of scripture and liturgy at the same time that we begin, through the shock of dissimilar symbols, to recognize that we must surpass the material level to reach the conceptual, and eventually even the supra-conceptual, level of meaning. On the conceptual level, in which we ascribe names to God, we also begin to learn that all conceptual signification must be abandoned in order to appreciate the real depths of the dissimilarity that alone leads to God. It is here that Dionysius's special contribution to the history of negative theology is to be found. The Areopagite insists on the superiority of negation over affirmation in all ways of referring to God. All predicates, however exalted, must be stripped away from God because none of them does justice to his transcendent perfection. As he says:

Now it seems to me that we should praise the denials quite differently than we do the assertions.... As we

climb from the last things up to the most primary,
we deny all things so that we may unhiddenly know
that unknowing which itself is hidden from all those
possessed of knowing amid all beings. (*MT* 2)

What exactly is this unknowing that Dionysius praises so
highly? Obviously, it is not a "what" at all, not some concept
or content that can be described or defined. It is more like
a state of mind — the subjective correlative to the objective
unknowability of God. It can only be spoken about through
paradoxical assertions of contraries: "And this quite positively complete unknowing is knowledge of him who is above
everything that is known" (Letter 1).

Unknowing, Union, and Ecstasy

Dionysius has two ways of speaking about unknowing, based
on his distinction between symbolic and rational theology.
In the first mode, mystical theology in the proper sense lies
beyond all images and names and therefore cannot be spoken
or written about. But mystical theology *as written* (improp-
erly) is constructed through the aid of symbolic theology
and rational theology, which lend the mystical theologian
terms from the worlds of symbolic and conceptual discourse
that are used in transferred senses in order to suggest what
lies beyond all speech. From the world of symbolic discourse
Dionysius takes the language of darkness, cloud, and silence
drawn from the account of Moses' ascent to meet God on
Sinai (Exod. 19–20) to provide metaphorical descriptions of
attaining the hidden God. Moses is the model of one who,
breaking free of all seeing, "plunges into the truly mysti-

cal darkness of unknowing" (MT 1.3). In appealing to the story of Moses' dark encounter with God, Dionysius was not inventing the mysticism of darkness, which had a tradition going back to Gregory of Nyssa and beyond to the Jewish philosopher and mystic Philo of Alexandria. The Areopagite uses the theme of negation in an objective sense to signify God's utter unknowability, an unknowability that indicates that we attain God only through unknowing. In later mysticism, such as in the famous *Cloud of Unknowing* of the fourteenth century, we find this theme developed with more subjective uses.

The second mode of using language to suggest what lies beyond it is more complex. Dionysius asserts not only that God is unknowable, but also that God is "more than unknowable" (MT 1.1). What can this mean? Dionysius teaches that while negation is superior to affirmation in the anagogic process, *both* affirmation and negation need to be surpassed to reach final union with God. Within its undifferentiated unity the Trinity holds "the assertion of all things, the denials of all things, [and] *that which is beyond every assertion and denial*" (*DN* 2.3–4). That God lies beyond both affirmation and negation is the final message of the great hymn of negations that concludes the *Mystical Theology*:

> It is beyond assertion and denial. We make assertions and denials of what is next to it, but never of it, for it is both beyond every assertion, being the perfect and unique cause of all things, and, by virtue of its pre-eminently simple and absolute nature, free of every limitation, beyond every limitation; it is also beyond every denial. (MT 5)

More than any other patristic author, Dionysius used language (a very special language of his own) to subvert the claims of language — a position that has remained controversial down to the present.

The issues surrounding the meaning of unknowing should not blind us to the fact that it is not unknowing as such but union that is the goal of Dionysian anagogy. Dionysius claimed that his teacher Hierotheus attained "mystical union" with divine things (*DN* 2.9); he advises "Timothy" to "leave behind everything perceived and understood...to strive upward as much as you can to union with him who is beyond all being and knowledge" (*MT* 1). Dionysius insists that the believer achieves the goal of union within the liturgical context, as we have seen. Though our author does not expatiate on the nature of union, he does make it clear that union with God is to be thought of in terms of divinization, which "consists of being as much as possible like and in union with God" (*EH* 1.3).

Divinization is the gift that God bestows on beings endowed with reason and intelligence through their participation in the hierarchies. In identifying union with divinization, Dionysius was tying his new form of dialectical mysticism to what had already become a standard theme in Christian thought. For Dionysius the soul is divine and can achieve a form of indistinct union with God, but it is divine only as a *manifestation* and is unified and divinized only by God's uplifting eros. Divinization is a gift, not a birthright.

For Dionysius contemplative union is rooted in the ability to behold the thearchy through the hierarchy of creation. On the symbolic level it is insight into scriptural symbols and liturgical actions by means of which we can pass from mere material presentations to inner meanings. Within the ecclesiastical and celestial hierarchies, each level has a proper contemplation, which is directed to the next higher stage, up to the enlightenment given from above in the contemplation of the divine names. This is the second, or illuminative stage in the Dionysian itinerary. It is surpassed on the perfecting level of union in the "dazzling darkness of hidden silence" (MT 1.1), where all sensible and intellectual contemplation must be forsaken in the passage into darkness. Yet even here there will be an effort to see things that are seen in not being seen, contemplations that pertain to the unknowing that is the only true knowing of God.

Dionysius used language (a very special language of his own) to subvert the claims of language — a position that has remained controversial down to the present.

Ecstasy marks the transition to the place where all values are transmuted — both reversed (ignorance becomes knowledge, darkness becomes dazzling) and transcendentalized by passing beyond *both* affirmation and negation. Ecstasy effects this radical rupture through the power of love, the divine Eros implanted in the world through the ecstasy of God. It is through ecstasy that we pass beyond the human condition and become divinized. Paul, Dionysius's apostolic teacher, is the model:

This is why the great Paul, swept along by his yearning for God and seized of its ecstatic power, had this inspired word to say: "It is no longer I who live, but Christ who lives in me" (Gal. 2:20). Paul was truly a lover and, as he says, he was beside himself for God (2 Cor. 5:13), possessing not his own life but the life of the One for whom he yearned, as exceptionally beloved. (*DN* 7.13)

Thus, Dionysius's conception of union with God is based on a transcendentalizing of knowing into unknowing and of yearning eros into ecstatic possession. Both love and knowledge have essential roles. Dionysius's profound treatment of the names of God, that is, the attributes revealed in scripture and in rational exploration of the universe, give his mysticism a decided intellectualist cast. But love is never absent either. It is true that Dionysius's language of eros is not couched in the sexualized intersubjective imagery of the Song of Songs, but in the objective analysis of eros as a metaphysical principle. This does not lessen his contribution to the history of love in Western Christian mysticism.

CONCLUSION

The importance of the Areopagite lies in the fact that with him theology first became explicitly mystical, that is, he created the categories (including "mystical theology" itself) that enabled later Christian mystics to relate their consciousness of God's presence and the mystery of his absence to the tradition of the apostolic teaching represented by "Dionysius." Our mysterious writer was to remain the master of theology in its mystical incarnations at least in part because later mystics found in his writings the principles by which their lives and experiences could be understood both as expressions of and as essential to the divinizing action of the church's life.

No one knew better than Dionysius the limits of words in the face of the true mystery. As contemporary readers we may not find resonance with the complex interactions of the hierarchies, but we cannot fail to be moved as he describes reality as a beautiful circle of longing love, nor when he tells us that it is only in and through immersion in the beauty of the universe that we can discover that God is always more than we can conceive. We can also appreciate the way Dionysius draws us into participation in the life of Christ both by way of imitation and by participation in the liturgy. Most of all, however, we can feel in ourselves the longing involved in the pull into the divine darkness where "What is to be said of it remains unsayable; what is to be understood of it remains unknowable" (Letter 3).

SUGGESTIONS FOR FURTHER READING

The best translation of the Dionysian corpus in English is *Pseudo-Dionysius: The Complete Works*, translated by Colm Luibhead, Classics of Western Spirituality (New York: Paulist Press, 1987). A superb theological evaluation of Dionysius is found in the chapter devoted to "Denys" in Hans Urs von Balthasar, *The Glory of the Lord: A Theological Aesthetics*, vol. 2: *Studies in Theological Style: Clerical Styles* (San Francisco: Ignatius Press, 1984). Other useful works on Dionysius include Andrew Louth, *Denys the Areopagite* (London: Geoffrey Chapman, 1989); Paul Rorem, *Pseudo-Dionysius: A Commentary on the Texts and an Introduction to Their Influence* (New York: Oxford University Press, 1993);

and Hieromonk Alexander (Golitzin), *Et Introibo ad Altare Dei: The Mystagogy of Dionysius Areopagita, with Special Reference to Its Predecessors in the Eastern Christian Tradition* (Thessalonica: Analecta Vlatadon, 1994). On the wider issue of apophatic mysticism, see Denys Turner, *The Darkness of God: Negativity in Christian Mysticism* (Cambridge: Cambridge University Press, 1995), which treats Dionysius in chapter 2.

Ten

Cosmic Unification
JOHN THE SCOT

LIFE AND SIGNIFICANCE

Johannes Scottus Eriugena, or John the Scot, was born in Ireland about 810. We do not know where he studied in Ireland, but by the time of his arrival at the court of the Frankish emperor, Charles the Bald, about 845, he was already a very learned man for the times, a polymath who knew the liberal arts, astronomy, and medicine, as well as philosophy and theology. He became a close adviser to the emperor and was deeply involved in the theological debates of the day. About

191

860, Charles asked him to translate the works of Dionysius into Latin. After completing this task, he went on to translate other Greek theological texts. This encounter with Greek theology (unique in the early West) spurred him to compose a massive work of synthesis, the first true theological *summa* of the Middle Ages, which he called *Periphyseon,* or *On the Division of Nature.* In this work Eriugena sought to investigate the whole of reality, or nature, by, as he said, "working out a consensus" between the major theological sources of East and West. On the Western side, Augustine stands out as the main authority, but many other fathers and philosophers, such as Ambrose and Boethius, are also mined for their insights. On the Eastern side, Origen, Gregory of Nyssa, Dionysius, and the sixth-century monk Maximus Confessor are the dominant voices. John's *Periphyseon* was not just an encyclopedia, however, but a fundamental rethinking of the relationship between God and the cosmos. Much of the five books of *Periphyseon* is taken up with a long exegesis of the Genesis account of creation and fall. John's other major works are also commentaries: a homily and an unfinished exegesis of the Gospel of John, and an explanation of Dionysius's *Celestial Hierarchy.* The Irish scholar died shortly before 880 C.E.

John the Scot has long been hailed as the greatest speculative mind of the early Middle Ages, the most original and subtle philosopher-theologian in the West between Augustine and Anselm. His importance as an exegete has also recently been recognized. But why call him a mystic, given his lack of autobiographical witness to special experiences of God's presence? The determination of whether or not a particular author enjoyed what moderns refer to as mystical experience is difficult to make for many of the figures before 1200, because they rarely spoke in the first person about themselves. In our view this is not the key question to determine someone's place in the mystical tradition. Proceeding on the basis of the claim that mysticism is primarily an ecclesial tradition of prayer and practice designed to bring believers to a transforming awareness of God's presence, a good argument can be made that Eriugena played a key role in originating (or "erigenating," as James Joyce once punned) one of the most important traditions in Western mysticism, a form of Christian Neoplatonism later found in such mystical thinkers as Meister Eckhart and Nicholas of Cusa. For the Irishman the visible cosmos is a luminous manifestation, or theophany, of the hidden God. He sets out to show how the human mind mediates the return of the cosmos to the fullest possible union with God in the Divine Logos.

ERIUGENA'S DIALECTICAL VIEW OF GOD

Eriugena's teaching on God is an adaptation of the Neoplatonic dynamic view of the procession and return of all things out from and back into God as a way of understanding the Christian doctrines of creation and redemption. *Periphyseon* can be seen as a long experiment in expressing the inexpressible, that is, in using language in a way that shows its limitations are more important than its advantages in attaining God. In Book 1 of *Periphyseon,* following Dionysius, John distinguishes three modes of theology: the cataphatic, where we ascribe things to God; the apophatic, where we deny anything of God; and the language of eminence, or superessentiality, which dialectically fuses and thus

transcends both affirmation and negation because it is positive in appearance but negative in content. Eminent language
"says that God is not one of the things that are but that he
is more than the things that are, but what that 'is' is, it in no
way defines." Eriugena, like his predecessors in the dialectical tradition, especially Dionysius and Maximus, insists that
God is within the world as its deepest reality (a cataphatic
statement), but at the same time God is not of the world, but
apophatically above and beyond it. The language of eminence
tries to find formulations that will express how God is simultaneously and reciprocally always both within and beyond all
things.

> *"For everything that is understood and sensed
> is nothing else but the appearance of what is
> nonapparent, the manifestation of the hidden, the
> affirmation of the negated, the comprehension of
> the incomprehensible."*
>
> — John the Scot, *Periphyseon*

At the beginning of *Periphyseon* Eriugena defines nature
(*physis*), the subject of his work, as "the general name for all
things," comprising both the things that are and the things
that are not. To help understand the dynamic character of
nature, he divides this most general genus into four aspects
or species. The first is *that which creates and is not created*, i.e.,
God as the first cause. The second is *that which is created and
creates,* the divine ideas made within the Logos that are the
exemplars of our material universe. The species includes the
idea of humanity. Third is the universe itself, *the nature that is*

created and does not create; and the fourth species is *the nature that neither creates nor is created,* God as the hidden goal of all things. All four species are really aspects of God — God in Godself (species 1 and 4), and God as manifested (species 2 and 3). The cosmos as the manifestation of God is central to Eriugena's thought and his mysticism.

A favorite way in which John the Scot expresses God's positive relation to the world is taken from Dionysius — speaking of God as the essence of all things. This does not mean that Eriugena is a pantheist, because while God is the essence of all things, the converse is not true — all things are not God. God is infinitely beyond his creation. God in Godself is not really essence, being, goodness, or the like; but we can use these terms of God insofar as he makes the world and thereby manifests himself through it. The central negation of Eriugenean thought is that God is really Nothing, i.e., no-thing. "Therefore," he says, "the Divine Goodness, which is called Nothing for the reason that, being beyond all things that are and are not, it is found in no essence, descends from the negation of all essences into the affirmation of the essence of the entire universe — from itself into itself, as though from nothing into something" (*Per.* 3).

In the same third book of *Periphyseon* John presents a powerful series of nineteen dialectical antitheses to express the coincidence of negation and affirmation used when we speak of the universe as the manifestation of God. "For everything that is understood and sensed," he begins, "is nothing else but the appearance of what is nonapparent, the manifestation of the hidden, the affirmation of the negated, the comprehension of the incomprehensible, . . . " and so on. Each of the terms in the genitive points to the hidden God, while

the term in the nominative indicates God as both proceeding outward and then returning to Godself in the theophanic
universe.

THE COSMOS AS DIVINE
SELF-MANIFESTATION

Eriugena's dialectical view of God led him to an original
understanding of creation and the significance of the cosmos. If creation is nothing else than the manifestation of the
hidden God, then not only must God create out of himself
(i.e., out of Nothing), but it also follows that the fundamental nature of all created being is its function as manifestation,
that is, its ability to illuminate and reveal the hidden divine
nature. In book 1 of his commentary on Dionysius's *Celestial
Hierarchy* he says that "all the things that are, are lights."
He goes on to affirm how the cosmos as a whole is one vast
illumination:

> This is the reason why the entire fabric of this world is
> the greatest light put together from many parts as from
> lamps for revealing and beholding the pure reasons of
> intelligible things by the mind's highest power through
> the cooperation of divine grace and reason's aid in the
> heart of the wise and faithful.

In creation, the divine source "extends itself into all things
and that very extension is all things" (*Per.* 3). This extension is both self-negation and self-creation. God, as it were,
moves out from himself in a transformation that is designed
to reveal himself; and yet, at the deepest level, there is nothing "outside" God. In creation God comes to know himself,

that is, he realizes himself as the creative principle of the other. Creation, then, is "another God" in the sense that it is God manifested in otherness.

The language of light and darkness, widespread in scripture, is John the Scot's favorite way of speaking about this process of revealing and concealing. Light and darkness are often used as metaphors, but they are essentially more than that. Eriugena is a major exponent of what has been called "the metaphysics of light." The mutual reciprocity of light and darkness in our own experience of the world provides a phenomenological basis for seeking to understand the mysterious dialectic of God hidden and revealed — the more hidden the more revealed. The struggle to understand and express the relation between God and the world that is at the heart of *Periphyseon* can be experienced as simultaneously illumination and darkness. God in Godself is the dialectical coincidence of ineffable light and total darkness. When he reveals himself, it is as the "Father of lights" (James 1:17), a revelation grounded in the inner life of the Trinity, according to Eriugena.

The opening chapter of the *Commentary on the Celestial Hierarchy* shows how the "threefold light" of the Trinity, that is, the "first and interior light" of the Father, the "true light" of the Son, and the "gifting light" of the Holy Spirit, pervades the universe, "shining in all the things that exist so that it may bring them back into the love and knowledge of its beauty." All things are lights because they are created by the first light of the Father in his coessential light, the Word. Their essential function is to light our way back to God by revealing him to us. Even a stone or a piece of wood, properly understood, is a light, Eriugena asserts.

The role of the Word, or Creative Wisdom, the Second Person of the Trinity, is central to Eriugena's understanding of the creative process. Creation is not only the diffusion of invisible light in visible forms, but it is also the expression in manifest speech of the unmanifested Word of God. In a striking passage from the *Commentary on John*, Eriugena makes use of the analogy of creation as God's speech, or better, "shout" (*clamor*), to demonstrate the role of the Word both in procession and return. Commenting on John 1:23, "the voice crying out in the desert," he says:

> God's Word cried out in the most remote solitude of divine Goodness; its cry was the establishment of all natures. He called the things that are as well as those that are not, because God the Father cried out through him, that is, he created everything he wanted to create. He cried out invisibly before the world came to be in order to have it come to be; he cried out visibly when he came into the world in order to save it. The first time he cried out in an eternal way through his divinity alone before the Incarnation; afterwards he cried out through his flesh.

This passage highlights the role of the Word in procession and return. It is also the first text where the biblical motif of the desert solitude is used as a symbol for the hidden divinity.

God comes to know *what* he is in the act of creation, and creatures come to know *that* he is through the theophanic universe that illuminates and expresses him. The key to grasping how this reciprocal recognition takes place is in Eriugena's teaching about the relation between the Word of

God as Creative Wisdom and the Created Wisdom, which is the idea of humanity found in the second species of nature. Creative Wisdom stands at the beginning and end of the entire process of procession and return. As a passage from book 5 of *Periphyseon* says: "The universal goal of the entire creation is the Word of God. Thus, both the beginning and the end of the world subsist in God's Word, indeed, to speak more plainly, they are the Word itself, for it is the manifold end without end and the beginning without beginning, being without beginning save for the Father." The Word as Creative Wisdom is the "cause of causes," the divine center in which the second species of nature comes to be and in which all the ideas find their unity. "Christ who understands all things is the understanding of all things," and it is even possible to say that "the essence of all things is nothing else but the knowledge of all in Divine Wisdom" (*Per.* 2).

Among the primordial causes or ideas found in Creative Wisdom there is one that manifests God in a special way due to its own ability to know. This is the Created Wisdom, the idea of humanity, which Eriugena defines as "a certain intellectual concept formed eternally in the Mind of God" (*Per.* 4). All creatures are manifestations of God, but humanity in its ideal state reveals God in a unique way. Humanity is the true and only "image of God" (Gen. 1:26), because, like its divine source, it is capable of knowing. It is even more like God because it does not know *what* it is (essentially speaking, it is not a what, but a dynamic potentiality), but it does know *that* it is, namely, it possesses self-consciousness, just as God does in a transcendental way. Therefore, Eriugena's strong negative theology calls forth an equally powerful negative anthropology:

What is more wonderful and beautiful to those considering themselves and their God is that the human mind
is to be more praised in its ignorance than in its knowledge. For it is more praiseworthy in it not to know what
it is than to know that it is, just as negation is greater
and more consistent than affirmation in praise of the
divine nature. (*Per.* 4)

The consequences of this claim that human subjectivity
and divine subjectivity are essentially the same in their negation of concepts are startling. God himself is the subject (not
the object) of human knowing of God. In one place Eriugena
has God address us saying, "It is not you who understand
me, but I myself who know myself in you through my Spirit,
because you are not the substantial Light, but a participation in the Light that subsists through itself" (*Homily on
John*). From the perspective of creation, humanity as primal
cause, or Created Wisdom, has a correlative role to the Creative Wisdom of the Word in the procession of all things. As
self-conscious cause in the Mind of God, humanity knows,
actually in the second species of nature and potentially in
the third, all things in the universe. Thus, all things are created in it. Creation "occurs" in two places: causally, in the
Word, the Creative Wisdom; and effectively, that is, as things
made, in human knowing.

THE PATH TO UNION

The fall of humanity from its ideal status in the second species
of nature into the third species, i.e., the material universe
of multiplicity and distraction, is one of the most difficult

aspects of Eriugena's thought. Basically, his conception of the fall is both positive and negative: positive insofar as the third species still forms part of God's manifestation and the matter that characterizes it is not evil in itself; negative in the sense that the third species necessarily involves disharmony, exteriority, and especially illusion and ignorance in the minds of individual humans. These negative aspects can be overcome only by an act of redemption that is effected through the uniting of Creative Wisdom with Created Wisdom in the person of Jesus Christ, the Godman who incorporates all humans into himself and eventually will restore them to union with the Father.

The Eternal Word comes into our world of effects, the material universe, by taking on human nature "in which the whole world subsists." In his return to the Father, which begins through his dissolution in death on the Cross and his subsequent Resurrection seen as the beginning of the process of integration, he elevates the whole human race, and therefore the material universe that is contained in its knowing. This raising up takes place in two ways. First, all humanity, and therefore the cosmos, will eventually be restored to its pristine state in the idea of humanity as it exists in the second species of nature. In this sense, Eriugena, like Origen and Gregory of Nyssa, held to a universal view of salvation. But there will still be a significant distinction between the good and evil in the final state, according to John. Those who have followed Christ will be deified, that is, they will be conscious of their unified status; but the evil, who have not worked to overcome illusion and self-centeredness, will continue to be distracted by the sinful images they indulged in during life and will thus be ignorant of where they really are. Hell is nothing else than the continuing existence in the minds of the wicked of the fantasies of the things that misled them during their time on earth. What they regain in nature, they make themselves incapable of enjoying in their minds.

Such universal restoration, though realized in these two ways, can be achieved only through the saving action of the Word. As John puts it:

> In the Only-Begotten Word of God, incarnate and made man, the whole world is restored even now in its species, but at the end of the world it will return universally and in its genus. For what he specially wrought in himself, he will perfect generally in all: and not only in humanity, but in every material creature. (*Per.* 5)

But how is this return, so universal in scope, to be realized in our present life? Although Eriugena's cosmic mysticism is set forth in an intricately argued dialogue of many hundreds of pages, both *Periphyseon* and his shorter works indicate that he was attentive to more personal aspects of the application of his synthesis. John's treatment of the story of creation and redemption set forth in the Bible privileged the purely symbolic accounts that spoke, so to say, from the perspective of the ideal world of the second species of nature, but he never denied the basic facts of the history of salvation, especially the role of the mysteries of Christ's life.

The Resurrection has particular importance because it marks the overcoming of the sexual differentiation of male and female and the beginning of the absorption of the material reality of flesh into its higher state free from the constraints of space and time. The Ascension is the mystery that signifies how Christ has already begun the process of the

uplifting of humanity to the Father. Eriugena interprets the
Lord's reception into the clouds in the sight of the Apostles
(Acts 1:9–10) as the ascension he effects in his followers'
minds: "He really ascended in the contemplations of those
who are ascending with him — nobody can ascend to him
without him" (*Per.* 5). While John always directs his readers'
attention to the inner meaning, the spiritual reality, of the
mysteries of Christ's life and the sacraments of the church
that communicate these saving acts to us, it is their material
reality that makes them available to humans in a salvific way.

---

*Although John the Scot lived in a world long
before the rise of modern science, his sense of
the cosmos as a whole, a splendid manifestation
of the mystery whose light blinds us with delight
and desire, is still worth pondering today.*

John the Scot does not speak in personal terms of mystical union: his attention is centered on the general process
that makes the return possible for all humans. He lays out
a variety of stages of the return process that need not be
taken up here. Despite the universalism of his viewpoint,
however, Eriugena's writings contain some hints about how
he thought believers should endeavor to put the program of
return into effect in their lives. John follows Dionysius in
describing three stages of the uplifting activity that we must
begin in this life — "to be purged of all ignorance, illuminated
by all wisdom, and perfected by all deification" (*Commentary
on the Celestial Hierarchy* 10). John obviously thought that
his own contribution was to help overcome sinful ignorance

through the study of scripture and the church's teaching and the presentation of this message in a systematic form. There is almost no moral instruction in his writings, but he frequently speaks of the goal of the process, using the language of contemplation, deification, and union with God.

Deeply influenced by the Greek Fathers as he was, Eriugena speaks of deification more than any previous Latin author. Deification begins in this life, but will be perfected only after death. As he says in the *Commentary on the Celestial Hierarchy:* "We, indeed, still like little children, are being formed into the divine likeness within us by symbols and holy images, so that we may now be deified by this likeness through faith and afterwards will be deified in vision." Deification is defined in *Periphyseon* 5 as "the psychic and bodily transformation of the saints into God so as to become one in him and with him." It is clear from this text, and many other passages, that both contemplation of God and union with him can be participated in during this life, but will be completed only in the hereafter, at the end of time. Like many patristic authors, John analyzed the different forms of contemplation through a consideration of biblical prototypes, such as Elijah, Moses, Paul, John, and even Christ himself. He does not speak, except by implication, about how far these types of contemplation might be realized by his contemporaries. It was enough to know that the biblical models revealed where we should be headed.

John was also not much concerned with talking about union with God in the present. His attention is focused on the general union already begun in Christ and to be completed at the end, what he called "ineffable unification," or "ineffable union." His teaching here once again reflects the primacy of negation in his thought. Humanity's ultimate union with God discloses a state that both *is* and *is not* identity with God. There is an identity insofar as human nature will once again come to know fully that its self-consciousness is identical with God's. But that same realization will also be a deeper awareness of the always impenetrable mystery of God. John insisted that even in heaven God will be known by all intellects below the Intellect of the Divine Word not directly, but only through theophanies, even though they will be "theophanies of theophanies," manifestations undreamt of here below. The hidden God will never be completely revealed, nor known, nor contemplated. There is no final union or identity with the dark mystery — otherwise God would not be God.

The prayer that concludes *Periphyseon* expresses John the Scot's recognition of the partiality of all attempts to penetrate the mystery here below and a confidence that the light that shall be given us when reunification is fully achieved will both satisfy us and yet lead us ever onward in the divine darkness. Speaking of the difficulty of describing the return, he says: "Let everyone hold what opinion he will until that Light shall come which makes the light of the false philosophers a darkness and converts the darkness of those who truly know into light."

CONCLUSION

Although John the Scot lived in a world long before the rise of modern science, his sense of the cosmos as a whole, a splendid manifestation of the mystery whose light blinds us with delight and desire, is still worth pondering today. His desire for illumination was driven by the desire for the final goal, the face of God, the ultimate resting place for the human heart and mind.

SUGGESTIONS FOR FURTHER READING

For a complete translation of John the Scot's great work, see Eriugena, *Periphyseon (The Division of Nature)*, translated by I. P. Sheldon-Williams, revised by John J. O'Meara (Washington, D.C., and Montreal: Dumbarton Oaks and Bellarmin, 1987). John's important *Homily on the Prologue to John* is available in *Celtic Spirituality*, translated by Oliver Davies, Classics of Western Spirituality (New York: Paulist Press, 1999). A good introduction to the Irish thinker is Deirdre Carabine, *John Scottus Eriugena* (New York: Oxford University Press, 2000). Important monographs on John the Scot include Dermot Moran, *The Philosophy of John Scottus Eriugena: A Study of Idealism in the Middle Ages* (Cambridge: Cambridge University Press, 1989); and Willemien Otten, *The Anthropology of Johannes Scottus Eriugena* (Leiden: Brill, 1991).

Eleven

Spousal Love

BERNARD OF CLAIRVAUX

LIFE

In 1112 he entered the struggling new monastery of Citeaux with thirty companions. Thirty. No wonder it is said that mothers hid their sons and wives clung to their husbands at his approach. Bernard of Fontaines was a well-educated Burgundian nobleman born near Dijon, France, in 1090. At the age of twenty-two Bernard renounced his inheritance and set out to find Christ in solitude, silence, poverty, and a life of prayer. Three years after entering the Cistercian Order, he was a young abbot sent to found Clairvaux, "Valley of Light," the monastery ever afterward associated with his name.

Bernard of Clairvaux has been called the "difficult saint" mostly due to the ways he sometimes used his considerable personal and spiritual power to bully people into doing what he believed was the will of God. Bernard could be virtually impossible to resist on the personal level, sundering even happy marriages of his siblings and others whom he wanted to bring into his monastery. In pursuit of this agenda, he established a separate monastery for the wives who would release their husbands and go into religious life themselves.

On the political level, at the request of Pope Eugene III (one of his former monks), he preached the Second Crusade with great fervor but less political sense. The crusade ended in complete disaster. Bernard's role in it was criticized at the time and has been a problem for his admirers ever since. Despite the many difficult aspects of Bernard's personality and actions, the personal attractiveness and holiness of the man shines through all the accounts of his life. People loved him, were inspired by him, and wanted to follow him. In the end he established at least seventy monasteries to house the flocks of new recruits to the Cistercians. He died in 1153, famous as a contemplative, but also as a man of action, deeply involved with a wide range of the issues of his time. He had become the dominant figure of his age, leaving behind profound changes in the political, religious, and literary life of medieval Europe.

WRITINGS

The student of Bernard's mysticism is confronted with a wealth of riches. His writings include many sermons and letters, and a number of formal treatises, such as *On Consideration,* a text written for Pope Eugene III as a spiritual directory for all prelates; the *Apologia,* defending the Cistercians against the Cluniacs; and the *Steps of Humility and Pride,* which shows how the twelve degrees of humility demanded by the Rule of St. Benedict leads the monk to contemplation and to loving contact with God. *On Loving God* (1126–27), his central mystical treatise, expounds the abbot's view that the very nature of the human is to love, and that loving God is a person's main reason for existing. In this treatise Bernard lays out an itinerary of four degrees of love that is numbered among the most important descriptions of the path to loving union with God in the history of Christian mysticism.

Important as Bernard's treatises were, his reputation as a master of mystical teaching rests primarily on his *Sermons on the Song of Songs* (SCC), begun in 1135, eighty-six homilies that comprise a highly developed and richly rhetorical treatment of the mystical life cast as a spiritual exegesis of Solomon's song of love. Along with the four mystical treatises of John of the Cross, Bernard's *Sermons on the Song* can be said to be a true *summa,* or synthesis, of Christian mysticism.

Bernard the writer was, first and foremost, Bernard the preacher, that is, he preferred to cast his most important theological productions in the sermonic genre. Along with the *Sermons on the Song of Songs,* the *Sermons on the Liturgical Year* count as central to his teaching. These liturgical sermons center on the mystery of redemption as the communication of divine life to the church through her annual reliving of the saving events of Christ's life.

DOCTRINAL FOUNDATIONS

It is not possible to understand Bernard's mystical theology without grasping the main lines of his theological program. His sermons on the Song of Songs begin with eight sermons on the text, "Let him kiss me with the kisses of his mouth" (Song 1:2). These homilies center on the economy of salvation. According to Bernard, the mystery of our redemption in Christ can be realized only partially and imperfectly in this life. It will be fully realized at the resurrection of the body. Although all the sermons on the Song concentrate on the personal meaning of the text as telling of the love between Christ and the individual Christian, Bernard cannot help but turn again and again to the mystery of Christ and the church in which the personal relation is rooted. In order to grasp the mystical theory of the saint, therefore, we need to consider if only briefly his anthropology, Christology, and ecclesiology.

Bernard's Theological Anthropology

For the abbot of Clairvaux, our experience of life is one of an almost unbearable tension between what we were *meant to be* and *what we are* — between the grandeur and the misery of the human condition. The essential root of Bernard's anthropology, like that of all the fathers of the East and West, is based on the Genesis account of humanity's formation in the image and likeness of God (Gen. 1:26). Like many others, the abbot understood the text in terms of Paul's teaching that Christ is the perfect Image of the Father, the image to whom fallen humanity is reconformed through salvation. The existential starting point of Bernard's anthropology, the Christian adaptation of the Delphic maxim "Know thyself," was this recognition of our misery (our fallen condition) combined with our majesty (the possibility of restoration to the original image and likeness of God through the soul's bond with the Word).

The body, though it can weigh down the soul by the false loves of concupiscence, is central to Bernard's mysticism. He insists that our journey toward God must begin on the carnal, or bodily, level and that our enjoyment of bliss will not be complete until our physical bodies are reunited with our souls at the general resurrection. The effect of this honest recognition of our plight in the present is humility, the essential starting point of the spiritual life. Despite our sorry condition, we know that God "creates our minds to participate in him" (*On Consideration* 5.11.24), so that this self-knowledge also brings hope for a change in our condition, the first step in a lifelong process of conversion.

The humility and the hope that are the beginning of our journey away from sin and back to God do not come from our own effort, but are already the work of the Incarnate Word in us. The voluntary humbling of God in taking on flesh casts the lie in the face of all human pride. The merciful kindness Jesus displayed throughout his life is the source of hope for all sinners, no matter how hardened. Here theological anthropology joins Christology, the centerpiece of Bernard's doctrinal message.

Bernard's Teaching on Redemption

He offered his flesh to those who knew flesh so that through it they might come to know spirit too. While he

was in the flesh, through the flesh he performed works
not of the flesh but of God. (SCC 6.3)

The abbot helps us understand the message of humility
and mercy through his distinctive teaching on the "carnal"
love of Christ. For Bernard, Jesus, the Godman, is lovable on
the most basic level of human attraction, that of the flesh.
This is why he took on humanity, since he knew "if he had
not drawn near, he would not draw to himself, and if he had
not drawn to himself, he would not have drawn out of sin"
(*On Grace and Free Choice* 3.12). Carnal love of Christ in
the flesh, and "what Christ did or ordered in the flesh," form
the "main reason why the invisible God wished to be seen in
the flesh and to live among humans as a human so that he
might return all the affections of carnal humans, who could
only love carnally, first to the saving love of his flesh, and
thus, little by little, lead them to spiritual love" (SCC 20.6).
The sweetness of carnal love of Christ is needed in order to
drive out the false sweetness of illicit loves — as nail expels
nail (SCC 20.4).

The abbot of Clairvaux insists at the outset that carnal
love cannot be merely denied or rejected, but that it must
be accepted and redirected to the sensible or carnal love of
Christ's humanity, the necessary starting point on the road
to the spiritual love of his divinity. For Bernard such carnal
love was always just the beginning of the itinerary that was
meant to lead to spiritual love. To neglect the higher form
of love would be to fail to do justice to Bernard's thought.
This is why the Resurrection, and even more the Ascension,
were such special feasts for him. The transition from carnal
to spiritual love achieved in Christ risen and ascended is the

center of Bernard's Christology: "Christ ascended once and for all above heaven's height in corporeal fashion, but now he ascends every day spiritually in the hearts of the elect" (*Sermons on Different Topics* 61.1).

Both the will and the ability to pursue the way of salvation come from the Incarnate Word, the source of all our strength. Our conformation to the Word, a constant theme of Bernard's teaching, is our transformation into the perfected image and likeness as we, like Christ our Head, pass from the carnal to the spiritual level: "That carnal love through which the carnal life is excluded and the world is condemned and overcome is good. When it is also rational it advances; it is perfected when it also becomes spiritual" (SCC 20.9).

Bernard's Ecclesiology

Christian mysticism is necessarily corporate, that is, it takes place in and with the body of believers. Bernard is a strong witness to the ecclesiological basis of all union with God. The process of Christ's saving work, the restoration of humanity to the possibility of attaining its true goal, has as its immediate subject not the individual human person but the church, the collectivity that forms Christ's Body both here on earth and in heaven. "No one among us would dare to claim for himself the title of Bride of Christ for his soul, but because we belong to the church which justly glories in this name and its reality, we not unjustly appropriate a share in this glory" (SCC 12.11).

The abbot of Clairvaux was less interested in breaking new ground with this interpretation than in renewing the tradition of melding the ecclesiological and the personal reading of the Song after many centuries in which a largely church-related interpretation had predominated. Bernard's thoughts on the inner reality of the church as the Body of Christ in the history of salvation are integral to the doctrinal basis of his mystical theology. The true church is the preexistent reality of the heavenly Jerusalem. Although the Word had a Bride from all eternity in the angelic host, "It pleased him to call the church together from humanity and to unite it to the one from heaven, so that there might be one Bride and one Groom" (SCC 27.6). Bernard not only revived early Christian emphasis on the preexistent reality of the church, but his fusion of the angelic and human aspects of the church into one perfect Bride helps explain the important role that the angels play in his mystical theory. The total mutuality of love in the great sacrament of marriage between Christ and his Body the church establishes the foundation upon which the abbot constructs his mysticism.

BERNARD'S MYSTICAL THOUGHT

Bernard of Clairvaux's mystical theology, like all his thought, proceeds in exegetical fashion — the interpretation of the Song of Songs, the constant invocation of certain key scriptural texts, and, above all, his amazing ability to combine passages from the whole of the Latin Bible in his teaching. Two things should be noted about the structure of the Cistercian's mystical thought: the universality of its message and the dynamism of its view of the soul's progress. Bernard's emphasis on the universality of the call to contemplation contains a built-in tension. He certainly believed that salvation was offered to all Christians, and he implied that in theory all could aspire to the loving union with the Bridegroom in this life, but in practice Bernard seems to have thought that it was difficult, if not impossible, for anyone outside the monastery to attain the higher stages of loving union.

"No one among us would dare to claim for himself the title of Bride of Christ for his soul, but because we belong to the church which justly glories in this name and its reality, we not unjustly appropriate a share in this glory."

—Bernard of Clairvaux, *Sermons on the Song of Songs*

A second characteristic of Bernard's view of the call to the delights of loving God is the dynamic and progressive view he had of this invitation. His notion of the Christian life is that of a single grand continuum of love stretching from the earthly and carnal love of fallen humanity for Jesus to the heights of heavenly spousal love, a level at which progress comes very slowly. This prudent teaching about the necessity of gradual progression exists in tension with the impatience of vehement love that Bernard insists is never satisfied short of the highest experience of union with God. The coexistence of prudence and ardor gives the abbot's thought a special dynamism.

The Role of Experience

"Today we read in the book of experience," says Bernard as he begins his analysis of the personal meaning of the Song of Songs (SCC 3.1). He constantly insists that personal experience is necessary for his listeners to understand his message:

"In matters of this kind, understanding can follow only where experience leads" (SCC 22.2), a warning that gives the non-mystical interpreter pause. Several times Bernard makes bold to recount his own experience. In the seventy-fourth of his sermons on the Song of Songs he says:

> Now bear with my foolishness a little while (2 Cor. 11:1). I want to tell you as I promised about my own experience of this sort of thing. Not that it is important (2 Cor. 12:1), but I am relating it to be helpful. If you profit from it, I shall be consoled for my foolishness. If not, I will proclaim my foolishness. I admit that the Word has also come to me, and — I speak foolishly (2 Cor. 11:17) — come often. As often as he has come to me, I have not perceived the different times of his coming. I perceived that he has been present; I remembered that he had been there. Sometimes I was able to anticipate his coming, but I never felt it, nor his departing either. Even now I admit that I don't know whence he came into my soul and where he went after he left it, and by what way he entered and left. (SCC 74.5)

The Word is not perceptible to the exterior senses. If we ask where he is or whence he has come, Bernard says we can get no answer. The Word is no-"where," that is, he is not in any place. We are rather in him. His presence can be sensed, perceived or felt only by the happy individual "in whom that Word dwells, who lives for him, who is moved by him" (SCC 74.5). The abbot's test for authenticity of the visit of the Word-Bridegroom is not in terms of any external experience of either normal or paranormal kind, but is based on the effect that the Word has on one's manner of life through the kindling of reforming love. "As I said, it was only from the movement of my heart that I understood his presence" (SCC 74.6). Similarly, the mark of his departure is the lessening of love that leaves the soul that has had "such experience of the Word" with an ardent and increasing desire for his return. Love and desire are the keys.

Love as the Center of Bernard's Mysticism: Major Themes

The Priority of Divine Love. God is love (1 John 4:8). No text from the whole of scripture meant more to our Cistercian than this passage. Bernard thought that it conveyed the most that we can ever really know about God — and all that we ever need to know. "God also loves and has no other source save himself from which he loves. That is why he loves more ardently, because he does not so much possess love as he is love" (SCC 59.1). Love is the "law" of God's being: He cannot do other than love, though, of course, he loves from the complete and spontaneous freedom of his infinite nature.

Though Bernard, like most classical Christian theologians, could not conceive of a God who could change or be affected by what lay outside his own being, God could be moved from within by his love for his creatures. "God cannot suffer, but he can suffer *with*, he whose nature it is always to have mercy and to spare" (SCC 26.5). What this means in practice is that God's love always has priority over and is the source of all other forms of love. "In this is charity, not that we have loved God, but that he loved us first" (1 John 4:10) — another text that Bernard never tired of quoting. As the Bride comes to recognize that she is always both anticipated and surpassed in love, she is impelled to seek to grow in love more and more in order to respond to the generosity of her Divine Lover. Bernard puts it as follows:

> His beauty is his love, all the greater because it was prior. The more she understands that she was loved before being a lover, the more 'and amply she cries out in her heart's core and with the voice of her deepest affections that she must love him. Thus, the Word's speaking is the giving of the gift; the soul's response is wonder and thanksgiving. The more she grasps that she is overcome in loving, the more she loves. The more she admits that he has gone before her, the more awestruck she is. (SCC 45.8)

The Nature of Human Love. Bernard works to understand the dynamics of the way in which the love that has been planted in our nature, even when that love is curved in on itself in the selfishness of fallen humanity, calls out for its Maker and launches us on the path toward the heavenly joy and love that are its true goal. "God," he says, "is the reason for loving God; the measure of loving him is to love without measure" (*On Loving God* 1.1). The problem with fallen humanity is that we can no longer directly appreciate *why* God is the only real reason for loving God, nor can we understand *how* to love without measure. Fallen humans' unending desire for more and more finite objects to satiate their hunger presents a perverted image of the true unending love, the insatiable satisfaction which is the genuine love of God.

God's prior love meets the fallen creature on the only level on which it can be found, that of selfish carnal love. Hence the reason for the Word's taking on flesh. The abbot spells out the four degrees of love's education, beginning with the "carnal love by which a person loves himself for his own sake before everything" (*On Loving God* 8.23). If this love did not retain at least a shadow of its divine source, there would be nothing that could be done to transform it. Even carnal love is the use of a basically good appetite in a perverted way. The humble and selfless example of the Godman helps us expand and reorder our selfish love, first through the physical love of Christ and his works, and second, when our recognition of our neighbor's wretchedness leads us to moderate our own pleasures and come to each other's assistance.

The second degree of love, based on the recognition of the greatness of the love God has shown to his creature, stimulates a response in which the person loves God for what God has done for him or her. This stage can lead to the third stage of love, as Bernard elaborates:

When one sees that he is not self-sufficient, he begins to seek and to love the God he needs for himself through faith. Then he loves God in the second degree — not for God's sake, but for his own. But when, on the basis of his own need, such a person begins to adore and pay attention to God — thinking, reading, praying, obeying — God slowly and gradually becomes known in the form of acquaintance and so grows sweet. In this way, having tasted that the Lord is sweet (Ps. 33.9), the soul passes to the third stage in order to love God no longer for her own sake but for God's sake. It will surely be in this stage for a long time. I don't know if anyone perfectly attains the fourth stage in this life — that in

which someone loves himself only for God's sake. If anyone has experienced it, speak up! It seems impossible to
me. (*On Loving God* 15.39)

Bernard's rhetoric was always designed to help bring his
reader to the experience of God, and he was sure that the
primary way to achieve this was through the language of
bridal love.

Spousal Love. The four degrees of love, important as they
are for giving a sense of Bernard's general approach to how
love alone can unite us to God, are preparatory to the abbot's
most impressive teaching on love as a spousal relation to God.
Spousal love's superiority to all other loves appears every-
where in Bernard. Toward the end of the *Sermons on the Song
of Songs*, for example, he says:

> Love is a great thing, but there are degrees in it. The
> Bride is at the top. Children also love, but with thought
> to an inheritance. . . . I am suspicious of a love which
> seems to be supported by hope of gaining something
> else. . . . Pure love has no self-interest. Pure love does
> not take its power from hope, nor does it feel any kind
> of distrust. It belongs to the Bride, because this is what
> a Bride is. Her reality and her hope are one single love;
> she is rich in it and the Bridegroom is content with it.
> He is not looking for anything else; she has nothing else.
> (SCC 83.5)

This is how Bernard sums up the position of the Bride
and points to what defines her: the pure, disinterested, and
total character of her affection. God is what he has: God
does not possess love but is completely love. No creature can

ever attain this transcendent simple identification, but the Bride comes closest in her total absorption in loving without thought of self or reward. "Even though the creature loves less, because it is less, still if she loves from her whole self nothing is lacking where everything is given. Loving in this way, as I have said, is being married" (SCC 83.6). Spousal, or marital, love is thus pure or sweet love, but it has many other dimensions. It is wise and prudent, that is, not contrary to intellect and understanding, the higher dimensions of human knowing. It is also vehement and forceful in ways that may seem insane to those who have not experienced it. Such love is completely mutual, and it is also perfectly satisfying in the sense that it is the highest form of vision or contemplation of God and the most exalted type of union. Finally, it sets in order all the other affections of the soul. These characteristics of spousal love will provide the structure for the analysis that follows.

Pure love is love free of any thought of gain for the self. From the perspective of the Bride herself, love, if it is truly bridal love, *must* be its own reward: "It is its own merit, its own reward. Love has no cause or fruit beyond itself: its fruit is its use. I love because I love. I love that I may love" (SCC 83.4). Love, then, is the ultimate enjoyment of the Bride — her truest "sweetness" — because it is its own reward. From this viewpoint, the issue of what kind of "self-love" remains in pure love is clear. We love the "self" insofar as it has recovered its true reality in God, that is, as it is regaining the image and likeness of God. In its deepest reality, the soul is the created manifestation of the overwhelming divine love itself. Bernard would have thought us to be seriously failing to live the new divine life of grace if we were to try to exclude *all* love of ourselves (those selves for whom Christ died). The real issue for the abbot was in learning *how* we are to love ourselves in an unselfish way.

The abbot of Clairvaux accepted the major commonplaces of the Western Christian tradition, namely, that the capacities to know and to love were the essential aspects of human nature and that both powers, though injured by sin, shared in the gradual restoration of the divine likeness made possible by the saving work of Christ. Although he does not explicitly say so, it is clear that Bernard thought that the intellectual power was, if anything, more injured, more susceptible to pride, more tempted to rely on itself, even after grace had intervened, than the will. True knowledge, that is, the self-knowledge of humility, is as necessary to the foundation of the reformation of the intellectual side of human nature as the love of the flesh of Christ is to the affective side. Since the fall, intellect's self-dependence represents a block to reaching God; but the *cooperation* between intellect and love is still *necessary* for attaining the goal. Because "God is the Love" who is identical with Truth, the spousal love that attains him must involve a reformed intellect, one that grace makes wise, prudent, and even reasonable — as well as being sweet and violent. Both the intellect and the affections need to be purged so that we can know nothing but God and desire nothing save him (*Sermon on the Ascension* 3.1). Bernard was sure that both love and knowledge were indispensable for union with God, however great love's priority remained.

Love is not only rational-prudent-wise, that is, compatible with illuminated intellect; it is also forceful, powerful, even violent. What may seem like a paradox to the natural mind, Bernard would say, is something well known from the book of experience to those who have actually sensed the presence of the Bridegroom. God is a violent Lover and the Bride, in order to attain him, must "let go" with a similar violence. Bernard strove to inculcate vehement love in his readers. We should be driven by desire, not by reason: "Headlong love doesn't wait for judgment, isn't tempered by advice, restrained by shame, or subject to reason" (SCC 9.2). We should strive "to take love's kingdom by force" (SCC 27.11), to become subject to the intemperate love that drives us on and gives us no rest. Twelfth-century thought and literature, both secular and spiritual, frequently explored the theme of the violence of love. In his exposition of this aspect of spousal love, Bernard shows himself to be very much a man of his time when he says:

> "Have you seen him whom my soul loves?" (Song 3:3). O headlong love, vehement, burning, impetuous, which cannot think of anything besides yourself! You feel distaste for other things, condemning everything besides yourself in self-absorption. You mix up proper order, you leave ordinary usage unnoticed, you are ignorant of due measure. Everything that seems to belong to reason, shame, counsel or judgment you conquer in yourself and lead captive. Everything that the Bride thinks and speaks, sounds and smells of you and nothing else. You have claimed her heart and tongue for your own. (SCC 79.1)

The love relation of which Bernard speaks is a marriage, not a love affair, not least of all because it is founded on a mutuality and reciprocity between the lovers that finds its closest analogy in human marriage, at least human marriage considered in an ideal sense. In addressing the problem of how there can be mutuality between Creator and creature, Bernard explains that when both partners give their all and share as fully as they can in one and the same reality — that is, in love — even the infinite distance between Creator and creature is lost sight of in the unitive experience. Between spouses "all things are shared; they have nothing of their own, nothing to divide them" (SCC 7.2). Their love easily mingles because it comes from the same source (SCC 45.1), the mutual charity that is the bond of perfection. God himself is no exception to the law of love, which makes lovers not only equal, but actually one (SCC 59.2). This sharing, by which the Bride and Groom can be so perfectly directed toward each other in mental attitude, is based on the soul's reality as the image of God. As one important passage explains:

> Therefore, from what she possesses that belongs to God, the soul in love recognizes and has no doubt that she is loved. This is the way it is — God's love gives birth to the soul's love and his prevenient intention makes the soul intent, full of care for him who cares for her. I do not know what closeness of nature it is that enables the soul, when once his face is revealed, to gaze upon God's glory and to be necessarily so quickly conformed to him and transformed into the same image (2 Cor. 3:18). Therefore, in whatever way you get yourself ready for God, this is the way he will appear to you. (SCC 69.7)

Bernard's stress on how the Bride and the Groom find their delight in mutual interaction necessarily suggests the most intimately mutual act of spouses, sexual intercourse. Bernard tends to use marital intercourse more by suggestion than by description as an apt symbol for mystical union, drawing upon the texts in which the Bride is embraced by the Bridegroom (Song 2:6). This image of the embrace is perhaps the most important erotic image after the kiss in the abbot's writings.

Bernard conceived of mystical union in this life as a more immediate experience of God than anything else conceivable here below, but because it still requires some mediation, it lacks final satisfaction. As long as we are in this life, any attainment of union with God will be fraught with as much yearning as with satisfaction or rest, however ecstatic the brief moment of absorption into the unity of spirit. In this life we will be ever reaching out for what is ahead, and, even in heaven, we will be ever moving forward into the inexhaustible mystery of God. As we have already seen in Gregory of Nyssa, unending yearning accompanies the different forms of satiating union experienced in this life and the next.

Bernard was also deeply concerned with how spousal love orders all things. One sermon says:

> If we love the things that should be loved, if we love more the things that should be loved more, and if we do not love the things that should not be loved, love will be purged. It is the same with the other affections. They are to be ordered in this way — in the beginning fear, then joy, after this sadness, love as the consummation. (*Sermons on Different Topics* 50.2)

This is Bernard's definition of rightly ordered love. The whole of the Christian life should be an ordered manner of living and loving; the core meaning of our conformity with Christ is the ordering of love — putting all our affections and desires in the proper relation. Truly ordered love, for the abbot, is the fruit of the love and knowledge that flow from the inebriating, albeit brief, experience of the union of spirit that we are given in this life. The proper relation between action and contemplation is the most important fruit of ordered charity. While affective love always starts with the love of God, that is, contemplative experience, the welfare of our neighbor, especially the weaker and more needy, comes first. Affective charity orders all things hierarchically in relation to God.

Where this greatest of Cistercian mystics marks a new departure is in how he insists that what he says is based on his own experience: "I am telling you of what I myself have experienced."

In this mode of love we begin by tasting, or experiencing, God, not, indeed, as he is, but insofar as we are capable of this experience (SCC 50.6). In this "tasting God" we come to know ourselves and our neighbor as ourselves. We can love other humans in two ways: we love as ourselves all those who love God as we love him, and we love our enemies, that is, those who do not love God, in order that they may come to love him. The abbot prays, "Direct our actions as our temporal necessity demands and dispose our affections as your eternal Truth requires so that each of us may safely boast in you and say that 'He has ordered charity in me'" [Song 2:5] (SCC 50.8).

It is the symbol of the soul as both Bride and Mother that stands closest to the heart of Bernard's mystical theory. The Bride must abandon the bedchamber and the delights of loving union, no matter how sweet, when called to perform works of active love, that is, to fulfill the duties of maternal love. It is Bernard's conviction that all true contemplatives will prove the authenticity of their experience of God by the alacrity with which they submit to the constraints of the call to charity. "We learn from this that the sweet kisses are often interrupted due to the breasts flowing with milk. No one lives for himself but all should live for him who died for all" (SCC 41.6).

Love and Union. A preoccupation with union, especially as experientially described, was a new element in the mysticism of the twelfth century. The flowering of new modes of mysticism seeking to find more adequate modes of expression was the driving force behind the new linguistic and theological developments. Bernard clearly teaches that the experience of loving union with God cannot really be communicated in rational and discursive terms. Metaphors are stretched to the limit. Bernard's richest text on union is to be found in the seventy-first of the sermons on the Song of Songs, a sermon that also displays the Cistercian's most developed teaching on the spiritual senses. Bernard begins his treatment here with a consideration of how while Jesus ate at Mary and Martha's house he also fed his hosts interiorly. In the present the reverse is true: "But if you saw that for him to be fed is to feed, see if now perhaps, on the contrary, to feed him is to be fed" (SCC 71.4). The meaning of this puzzle becomes clear in the following section as Bernard explains how eating is to be understood as a metaphor for uniting with or being *in* the other person:

My penance is his food, my salvation is his food, I myself am his food. . . . I am eaten when I accuse myself; I am

swallowed when I am instructed; I am cooked when I
am changed; I am digested when I am transformed; I
am united when I am conformed. Do not be amazed at
this — he eats us and we are eaten by him the more
closely we are bound together with him. Otherwise, we
would not be perfectly united to him. If I eat and am
not eaten, it will seem that he is in me but I am not yet
in him; but if I am eaten and do not eat, he has me in
him, but he will not seem to be in me as well. There will
be no perfect union in one or the other. (SCC 71.5)

Bernard is careful to distinguish between the union brought
about by love between a human person and God and the
consubstantial union of the Father and the Son. "One who
adheres to the Lord is one spirit [with him]." This classic
passage from 1 Corinthians 6:17 became Bernard's signature
text for describing the manner of union found in the love-
commerce of the Bride and the Groom. He taught that union,
both in this life and the next, does not surpass perfect loving
union of wills and never involves any form of union of identity
or indistinction with God. Neither is there any "face-to-face"
vision of God in this life. "God is not so much seen as guessed
at, barely touched in a delicate manner, the soul is rapt and,
as if with the flash of a passing little spark, burns with love"
(SCC 18.6). The flash of union is rare and fleeting: "Sweet
the mingling, but brief the moment, rare the experience!"
(SCC 85.13). Thus does the abbot read to us from the book
of his own experience. In another place he says:

When a movement of love of this sort is experienced
so that the intellectual soul is drunk with love and forgets itself, becoming almost an empty vessel to itself, it

marches right into God, and, adhering to him, becomes one spirit with him. . . . I would call a person blessed and holy to whom anything such as this very occasionally, or even just once, was granted as an experience while still in this mortal life — and that in a rapture of scarce a moment's duration! (*On Loving God* 10.27)

CONCLUSION

St. Bernard offers remarkable resources to the contemporary reader who strives to express the inexpressible experience of God. Like his predecessors, both in the East and the West, Bernard knew the limitations of all that he said and tried to say with such passion and elegance. Where this greatest of Cistercian mystics marks a new departure is in how he insists that what he says is based on his own experience: "I am telling you of what I myself have experienced" (SCC 51.3), as well as in how he constantly appealed to his listeners and readers to measure his message against the book of their own experience. Bernard continues to invite us to read in the book of our hearts. This "difficult saint" was gifted and yet human. Because of this, rather than in spite of it, we can open our hearts to learn from him how to approach the God of Love.

SUGGESTIONS FOR FURTHER READING

A complete translation of Bernard's *Sermons on the Song of Songs* is available from Cistercian Publications of Kalamazoo, Michigan, in four volumes. The same series also has translations of most of the abbot's other writings, including the key mystical treatise, *On Loving God,* with an analytical commentary by Emero Stiegman (Kalamazoo, Mich.: Cistercian Publications, 1995). For an anthology, see *Bernard of Clairvaux: Selected Writings,* translated by G. R. Evans, Classics of Western Spirituality (New York: Paulist Press, 1987). Among the many works devoted to Bernard's mysticism, see especially Etienne Gilson, *The Mystical Theology of St. Bernard* (New York: Sheed and Ward, 1940); Jean Leclercq, *St. Bernard and the Cistercian Spirit* (Kalamazoo, Mich.: Cistercian Publications, 1976); *Thomas Merton on St. Bernard* (Kalamazoo, Mich.: Cistercian Publications, 1980); Michael Casey, *Athirst for God: Spiritual Desire in Bernard of Clairvaux's Sermons on the Song of Songs* (Kalamazoo, Mich.: Cistercian Publications, 1987); and M. B. Pranger, *Bernard of Clairvaux and the Shape of Monastic Thought: Broken Dreams* (Leiden: Brill, 1994).

Twelve

Living the Trinity

WILLIAM OF ST. THIERRY

LIFE

The two men, both ill, were convalescing in the infirmary at Clairvaux. Bernard, Cistercian abbot of Clairvaux, and his friend William, Benedictine abbot of St. Thierry, fell into an extended conversation about the soul. Bernard disclosed to William the personal significance that his experience had enabled him to draw from the Song of Songs. Like the famous conversation of Augustine and Monica in Ostia, this collo-quy was to have profound effects on the Western mystical

231

tradition. Some years earlier, around 1118, William had met Bernard, about ten years his junior, and had been overcome with love and admiration for the saintly young abbot:

> Going into the hovel which had become a palace by his presence in it, and thinking what a wonderful person dwelt in such a despicable place, I was filled with such awe of the hut itself that I felt as if I were approaching the very altar of God. And the sweetness of his character so attracted me to him and filled me with desire to share his life amid such poverty and simplicity, that if the chance had then been given to me I should have asked nothing more than to be allowed to remain with him always, looking after him and ministering to his needs. (*Life of Bernard* no. 12)

As early as 1124 William was importuning Bernard for permission to join the Cistercians. Bernard initially resisted, but in 1135 William was finally allowed to join a new Cistercian foundation at Signy near Reims as a simple monk. The hard life of the white monks caused the aging ex-abbot initial difficulties, but he soon came to enjoy the rich leisure that enabled him to produce his most important writings. William took up his last task in old age — researching and writing a life of Bernard, who was still living. William's work on the *Life* was incomplete when he died on September 8, 1148.

WRITINGS

Because William was a friend and admirer of the great abbot of Clairvaux, his thought can be compared to Bernard's in many areas; but the fact is that the abbot of St. Thierry is very much his own man — an independent and powerful theorist of mysticism. His deeply personal *Meditations* were begun while he was still in his Benedictine monastery and were finished after he became a Cistercian. Augustine was the main source for his theology, but he was also versed in other patristic sources, especially Origen, Gregory of Nyssa, and Gregory the Great. As abbot of St. Thierry he composed his earliest works, *On Contemplating God* and a treatise on the nature and dignity of love. From about 1137 to early 1139 he worked on his *Exposition on the Song of Songs,* which was left unfinished while he undertook to refute the errors he saw in the writings of Abelard. Even so, the *Exposition* is arguably his greatest work. William divides the Song of Songs into four shorter poems or songs (1:1–2:7, 2:8–3:5, 3:6–8:4, and 8:5–14). He says that he is giving only a "moral" interpretation of the book, that is, one that concentrates on the personal application in which the Bride is read as the soul, rather than the allegorical, or doctrinal, reading interpreting the book as disclosing the mystery of Christ and the church. William's main attention centers on his understanding of loving union in the Holy Spirit.

In the early years at Signy William completed two important background works to his mystical compositions. The first was the *Nature of the Body and Soul,* in which he constructed an anthropology based on the harmonization of images — the human body as image (microcosm) of the universe, and the human soul as the image and likeness of God. The second was his *Exposition on the Epistle to the Romans,* a doctrinal sketch of the basis of his mystical theory. Sometime after 1140 he composed the joint treatises, *Mirror of Faith* and

Enigma of Faith. These contrast the two modes of knowledge (see 1 Cor. 13:12): our knowledge of God here below (as in a mirror); and the face-to-face vision to be enjoyed in heaven. This contrast forms one of the central themes of William's thought, designed to instruct his fellow monks on the proper understanding of the role of faith in the path to union with God. The *Mirror* treats that version of the path that leads from faith directly to mystical contact, and the *Enigma* elucidates the path that advances by applying reason to faith. While the *Mirror* is more overtly mystical than the *Enigma*, the two treatises taken together provide a full grasp of William's understanding of the relation of reason, faith, and love in the quest for the face-to-face vision of God.

"Be totally present to yourself, and make total use of yourself and whose image you are so that you discern and understand what you are and what you can do in him whose image you are."

— William of St. Thierry,
Exposition on the Song of Songs

The most popular of William's works is the *Golden Letter*, written in 1144. In a sense it is the treatise that Bernard should have written but never did — a perfect guide to monastic mysticism, as balanced as it is profound. The basic structure proceeds from the "animal" state of beginners in book 1, to the "rational" and "spiritual" levels of more advanced souls in book 2. The former abbot's strict and astute teaching, coupled with the profundity of his views on the mystical goal, make the *Golden Letter* one of the most important summaries of medieval mystical teaching. It was to have great influence in late medieval mysticism.

WILLIAM'S ANTHROPOLOGY

Like other monastic theologians, William based his mystical teaching on the fact that humans were created in the image and likeness of God:

> O Lord our God, who created us to your image and likeness, that is, to contemplate you and to enjoy you whom no one contemplates to the level of enjoyment save insofar as he is made like you, ... free from the slavery of corruption that in us which ought to serve you alone: our love. Love, when it is free, is that which makes us like you to the extent that we are drawn to you by that living perception by means of which whoever lives from the Spirit of Life has knowledge of you. (*Exposition on the Song of Songs* no. 1)

This passage from the beginning of William's *Exposition* can serve as an introduction to the major aspects of his mysticism. The constellation in which William puts these ideas from the rich tradition of Christian spiritual teaching gives us a hint of the special character of his mysticism.

William's anthropology outlines what it means for humanity to be made in the divine image and likeness. To be an image of anything means to participate in it, that is, to receive reality from it, but also to be distinguishable from it in some way. In William's theology the two terms "image" and "likeness" imply different but related forms of participation in God.

Image is the participation that comes from being created by God. This *originating participation*, based on creative grace, is the essential or original share in the divine nature that makes each person open to God — a form of participation that cannot be lost, though it can be damaged. Likeness, or resemblance, is the *perfecting participation;* it is the activity by which we come to resemble God in how we love and act. Though both forms of participation have been damaged by sin, the effect on likeness has been far more devastating: this participation has been lost.

For William the most important aspect of our *originating participation* in God is the human dignity of being an image of the Trinity. "The holy soul is reformed to the image of the Trinity," he says, "to the image of him who created her in the very manner of his beatitude. For a will that has been enlightened and drawn — that means intellect, love, and the disposition of enjoyment — is in a certain way three personal affections, as is said and believed of God the Trinity" (*Meditations* 12.14).

Almost all of William's explorations of the intricacies of the Trinity are directly related to how the soul as the image of the Trinity is to regain its lost likeness through the life of prayer and contemplation. As he says, "Be totally present to yourself, and make total use of yourself and whose image you are so that you discern and understand what you are and what you can do in him whose image you are" (*Exposition on the Song of Songs* no. 66). Thus, as William calls souls to the task of self-knowledge, he teaches that the deepest form of self-knowledge, beyond the initial recognition of our sinfulness and need for reform, is the gradual awareness of the mystery of our relation to the Trinity.

Sin has destroyed the resemblance, the likeness that is the *perfecting participation* that God gave us originally in creation. The way in which we regain the likeness to God in gradual and imperfect fashion during this life and perfectly in heaven is the whole content of William's mystical theology. One of the Cistercian's most noted texts concerning the divine likeness occurs toward the end of the *Golden Letter*:

> This is their [i.e., humanity's] whole perfection — resemblance to God. Not to wish to be perfect is to fall into sin. The will must always be nourished, love always prepared for the sake of perfection. The will must be restrained lest it lose itself in alien concerns; love protected lest it be sullied. It is for this alone that we were created and live. We were created to God's image so that we may be like God. (*Golden Letter* no. 259)

As the human will becomes more and more conformed to the divine Will, the soul's participation as a likeness to God moves in three stages, going beyond the soul's vivifying of the body to a higher form of likeness in the life of virtue, and ultimately into something more than a likeness, a unity of spirit. But we also become more like God as we come to know him or see him more directly. Though the full realization of the identity of vision and likeness remains for heaven, it must begin in this life. In the *Enigma of Faith* William reveals the divine ground for the dynamic identity of seeing and similarity:

> Just as in the Trinity, which is God, the Father and the Son see each other, and their seeing each other is for them to be one and for each of them to be what the other is, so those who are predestined to this and who

have been lifted up into it will see God as he is and in seeing will be made as he is, that is, like him. There, just as in the Father and the Son vision is the unity itself, so too in God and humans the vision is that future likeness. The Holy Spirit is the unity of the Father and the Son; he is also the charity and likeness of God and humans. (*Enigma of Faith* no. 6)

To love perfectly so that one is actually unable to love what God does not love, to see perfectly with the vision that constitutes the mutual knowledge of the Father and the Son, is the perfection of the likeness to God and the total fruition or enjoyment of the soul. This is the perfect likeness to be attained in heaven. William makes clear that in the journey of this life, love and reason, the soul's two essential powers, must work together to effect the restoration of our lost likeness. The Holy Spirit, working within the soul's natural powers by means of perfecting, or illuminating, grace, makes possible the ultimate transformation in which mystical loving and mystical knowing unite, and in this mutuality of love and reason the human person comes to the stage where love becomes understanding. This grace is the special divine gift whose purpose is to begin the restoration of the likeness to the Trinity that is meant to crown the image in the human soul. Hence living *in* the Trinity is the essence of William's mysticism.

THE DYNAMICS OF PROGRESS

To describe how believers advance to this participation in the life of the Trinity, William generally speaks of three stages of spiritual progress. First are those Christians who have faith, but are moved by authority, reminded by doctrine, and inspired by example to approve what is good where they find it. At a higher level are those who have begun the move toward interior religion: the soul is becoming more than just the vivifying power of the body. The intellectual soul becomes directed to the God who dwells within. In the third stage, spiritual souls "are the perfect who are led by the Spirit, who are more fully enlightened by the Holy Spirit. Because they taste the God whose attraction draws them, they are called wise. Because the Holy Spirit puts them on, . . . they are called 'spirituals' insofar as they are the clothing of the Holy Spirit" (*Golden Letter* no. 43). This divinely bestowed spiritual stage has its fruition in our unity of spirit with God. The transition from the first to the second stage is primarily (though not solely) understood as the work of the Incarnate Word, while the soul's lifting up to the spiritual stage is ascribed to the indwelling Holy Spirit.

In his commentary on the Song of Songs (*Exposition* nos. 88–106, commenting on Song 1:14–16), William sketches the anthropological foundation of the journey to union. The human person's essence as image and likeness of God consists in the Augustinian interior trinity of memory-understanding-love, understood as powers capable of being gradually directed to the God who alone is the soul's perfect fruition. Through these three powers the soul can attain the goal of full understanding, in which the spiritual intellect dominates all activities. She is then truly a Bride: "For the Bride, the memory of the Bridegroom is seeking him in simplicity of heart; understanding is thinking of him in goodness; love is being drawn to him, enjoying him, existing in the way that he does" (*Exposition on the Song of Songs*

no. 89). When the Groom finds the Soul-Bride in this condition, with what has been discolored by sin in her repainted
through the action of illuminating grace, he greets her as his
"beautiful one." The "eyes that are like doves" (Song 1:14)
signify reason and love, the two eyes of contemplation which
work together when enlightened by grace. Indeed, these two
eyes become one, "when in the contemplation of God, in
which love is chiefly operative, reason passes over into love
and is formed into a kind of spiritual or divine understanding
which surpasses and absorbs all reason" (*Exposition on the
Song of Songs* no. 92).

The matching beauty of the Bride and Groom enable them
to hold sweet conversation in which "they begin to taste the
joy of mutual joining." This converse, which is what leads the
soul to the measure of perfection that will be granted to it in
this life, is one in which the Groom speaks by means of operative grace and the Bride's response is the devout affection or
joy that she feels in her good conscience. God truly "speaks"
(that is, acts) in all souls, no matter how perverse; but he
speaks especially in the Bride when she is one spirit with him
(1 Cor. 6:17). "Such a one in her own way, according to the
power of faith, the light of understanding and the measure of
love, exists in God through grace as what God is by nature"
(*Exposition on the Song of Songs* no. 94).

This oneness of spirit is a sensible or perceptible experience, at least in a transferred sense. William bases his
explanation on the model of sense experience to emphasize
the reality, even the concreteness, of the knowledge of God
given in mystical experience. Moreover, there is a mutuality
to the experience by which God and human are joined "on
our little flowery bed," that is, within the human conscience.

"In it takes place that wonderful joining, that mutual enjoyment of sweetness and incomprehensible joy — unthinkable even to those in which it takes place — the conjoining of human to God, of created to Uncreated Spirit" (*Exposition on the Song of Songs* no. 95). Drawing out the trinitarian and Spirit-centered aspects of the joining, William says that what is realized in the soul (the image of the Trinity) is "the unity of the Father and the Son, their very kiss, the embrace, the love, the goodness and whatever is common to both of them in that supremely simple union. That is entirely the Holy Spirit, God, Charity, both Gift and Giver" (ibid.).

Just as human lovers share their breath or spirit in a kiss, "the created spirit pours itself out wholly for this purpose to the Spirit that creates it, and the Creator Spirit pours itself into the created spirit as it wishes and makes the human person one spirit with God" (ibid.). Of course this experience is always brief and intermittent in this life and is fully realized only in heaven. It is also the work of the entire Trinity, though one especially ascribed to the action of the Holy Spirit. God the Father, the source of all goodness, has not left us orphans. The Good Father is himself the love of those who love him. This love is nothing other than the Holy Spirit.

In this extended interpretation of Song 1:11–16 William develops his understanding of how love gradually absorbs reason and leads us to the unity of spirit in which we *become* the Holy Spirit, the very oneness of the Father and the Son.

Whereas Bernard knew that love was a form of understanding, William tries to probe how this is so. The abbot of Clairvaux recognized that our union with God is union with the entire Trinity, yet his mysticism is primarily Christocentric. William dwells more on the action of the entire

Trinity, centering his attention on the role of the Holy Spirit. These are differences in emphasis, not in fundamental belief; but they are important differences for all that.

ASPECTS OF WILLIAM'S TRINITARIAN MYSTICISM

Christ and the Economy of Salvation

William believed that in the divine plan of creation the universe would house human subjects formed in the image and likeness of the Trinity, and that the Word was from all eternity predestined to take on flesh as the Head of the Body of all those destined to be united with God. The Word's appearance in the flesh is designed to disclose the divine mystery to humanity. The goal of the descent of the Word into human life is the revelation of the mystery of God to humankind — something that love can experience, but human knowledge cannot attain. William, like Bernard, teaches that the carnal love of Christ is the necessary starting point in the movement toward truly spiritual love. William expresses his devotion to the Savior as the mediator who brings God's graciousness to humanity and humanity's faith to God. His is a Passion-centered piety that invokes the universal desire for the vision of God — that is, the manifestation of the face of God — as the deepest meaning of the mystery of the cross. The abbot recognizes that it is through the image of the Passion that our thoughts about God's goodness are transformed into a love for this goodness. In one of his *Meditations* he says:

> She [the soul] seems to see you as you are while she ponders your goodness toward us in her sweet

thoughts about the wonderful sacrament of your Passion. This goodness is as great as you are — it is what
you are. She seems to see you as you are, face to face,
when as the face of supreme Goodness you appear to
her on the Cross in the midst of your saving work.
(*Meditations* 10.7)

Love and Intellect

The Gregorian formula "love itself is a kind of knowing" is
important in William's mystical program. For the abbot there
are three moments in love's path: striving or desiring; feeling
or perceiving; and transformation. The ascent to God consists
of a whole series of motions or desires placed in us by God
that all work together, not like separate rungs of a ladder,
but more like the united cords of a net drawing us to our
goal. It is in the cooperative activity by which God draws us
and we let ourselves be drawn that the mutual indwelling
of Christ and the believer effects the transformation of the
soul from the animating spirit to the intellectual soul. On a
higher, totally passive level, the Holy Spirit draws us up to
the transformation of the intellectual soul into the spiritual
soul, the union of spirit by which we become the Love that
he is. William, like Bernard, insisted that we can love God
only because he has loved us first. All true love is God's love.
The definition of a Bride is that she "loves you only through
you who are the very life by which she loves you; she loves
you to such a degree in herself that she doesn't love herself
at all except in you" (*Exposition on the Song of Songs* no. 54).
So passionate a love is this that William, like other twelfth-
century mystics, though more sparingly, is willing to speak
about it as a form of insanity.

William describes the way in which the gift of divine love attains the level of feeling or perception. His overriding concern is to try to show how love, by the action of the Holy Spirit, is lifted up and transformed into an experimental knowledge of God that conveys a real, if nondiscursive, understanding of the Trinity. Sometimes William stresses the directness and connaturality of this knowledge (for this he uses the term *sensus amoris*), and sometimes he underlines that it is a real knowing, the kind of knowing that is signified in the famous formula cited above. For this he uses the term *intellectus amoris*. Transformative love, then, is both a *sensus amoris*, by means of which we concretely, almost tactilely, perceive or "feel" God, and also an *intellectus amoris*, by which we come to know him in a new way. In mystical union love can be transformed into understanding.

The Cistercian underlines at least three points about the nature of the transformation of love that takes place when the soul not only loves God with burning desire but also has begun to sense or perceive him. The first is that love of this kind advances beyond the boundaries of ordinary reason in its pursuit of God. This is not because reason is evil but because it is radically insufficient in the face of the divine infinity. Thus, it is necessary for reason to retreat or withdraw at a certain stage in the advance to God. This humility of reason does not mark its death or disappearance; rather, the voluntary withdrawal is what allows reason to be subsumed or lifted up to the higher level of knowing that William usually calls understanding, *intellectus*.

The Cistercian's second point emphasizes the mutuality of love and knowledge in this highest stage. The image of the embrace of the Divine Lover is one of William's favorite ways of expressing this mutuality of love and knowledge:

> The Bride's head is the heart's core warmed by the Groom's left arm (Song 2:6). This happens when a well-disposed mind enjoys that which it loves through the understanding of its own love. Thus each cooperates with the other for the good. While love strengthens reason so that it can be drawn along, reason does the same for love so that it can be embraced. Love is protected by reason, reason illuminated by love. Yet more, reason "effects" love and love "affects" reason by a prevenient grace that predestines, chooses, and calls. (*Exposition on the Song of Songs* no. 136)

The notion of prevenient grace mentioned in this passage underlines the third point William makes regarding the understanding of love, the *intellectus amoris:* the fact that such a state is a pure gift, given by the Holy Spirit to whom and when he chooses. This knowing seems to indicate an interpenetration, not an identification, of love and knowledge in a suprarational or supradiscursive mode of knowing perhaps best described as connatural. William insists that in mystical knowing the same powers are at work as in ordinary human knowing, but that they operate in a new fashion because they are activated by the Holy Spirit. Understanding, the *intellectus* of *intellectus amoris,* is in fact the immediate presence of Truth himself, the Divine Word. Moreover, mystical knowing is always transformative knowing; it changes the person by altering the usual structure of the process of understanding. The intellect cooperates with the action of the Holy Spirit by forming loving contemplation, and the intention of the thinking subject becomes the joy of one who delights in God.

Like virtually all twelfth-century mystics, William was concerned with the ordering of love. The soul attains the ability to order all loves properly by passing through an intermediary stage of internal turmoil or disorder. The Bride finds the virtues needed for human relations — prudence, temperance, and justice — so out of joint that she wishes only to die and to be with Christ. She is not allowed this, and grace eventually draws her out of her confusion and helps her relate her love of God, of self, and of neighbor appropriately as part of the process of regaining the likeness to God. "True love of self and neighbor is nothing else but love of God" (*Exposition on the Song of Songs* no. 121).

Vision and Union

The path that leads to the likeness of God regained through the understanding of love is also a contemplative vision bringing us to ecstatic union with God. A key theme for William is "face-to-face" vision of God. For the abbot the face represents the inner personal reality of God and the human person. According to William, "To seek God's face, that is, his knowledge, 'face to face' as Jacob saw it (Gen. 32:30), is what the Apostle says: 'Then I will know as I am known. Now we see through a mirror and in a mystery, but then face-to-face, as it really is'" (1 Cor. 13:12). Face-to-face vision is a great eschatological hope, not a real possibility in any full sense for humans in our present condition. Nevertheless, the desire for a face-to-face experience of the divine presence, the need "to bring before the face revealing grace the face revealing a good conscience" (*Mirror of Faith* no. 103), highlights the true goal of all human striving. And yet, we would not be seeking God unless we had already found him or, better, unless he had already found us. Even though we do not feel or see his presence, the soul still has flashes of the experience of God. They heighten her desire for the vision that can be fully enjoyed only in heaven.

William invokes one of the key scriptural texts concerning the vision of God and its relation to the life of the Trinity: " 'No one sees the Father except the Son, and the Son except the Father' (Matt. 11:27). This is what it is to be the Father, that is, to see the Son, and to be the Son is to see the Father" (*Meditations* 3.6). But, as William noted, Matthew goes on to say that the Son can decide to reveal this vision consisting in mutual knowledge through his Will, that is, the Holy Spirit. William took this at face value: we are invited to enter the mystery of the absolute mutual vision/knowledge of Father and Son by means of that mutuality itself: the Holy Spirit!

Seeing God begins with a vision that is not really a vision but is God's invisible presence working within us by grace and by faith, not yet in an experiential and perceptible way. Gradually, God's action in our soul begins to become visible as we sense the effects of his grace. This gradual cleansing of the soul is an opening of the inner eyes by which God's prior seeing of us makes us more and more able to see him. Addressing God, William says:

> And so, You see her first and make her able to see You. Standing before her, You make her able to stand up to You until the mutual drawing together of You who have mercy and she who loves completely destroys the barriers of sin, the wall dividing You, and there

is mutual vision, mutual embrace, mutual joy and one spirit. (*Exposition on the Song of Songs* no. 155)

As this passage proves, for William the development of the ability to see God is one and the same as advancing in the love of God. Seeing is loving, and therefore everything that we have said about the dynamics of love is also applicable to the progress toward face-to-face vision.

> *William displays a speculative power of mind unmatched by any mystic of his time, especially in his analysis of the relation of love and understanding in the mystical path and in his understanding of the role of the Holy Spirit as our union with God.*

If seeing God is really loving and knowing God on a new level, it is also nothing more nor less than becoming God "though not in every way," as our Cistercian says. Our gradual recapturing of the lost likeness of the Trinity in this life is only preparation for the full likeness to be attained in heaven. "To be like God there will be to see God or to know God. He who will see or know will see or know him to the extent that he will be like him. To see or know God there is to be like him, and to be like him is to see or know him" (*Mirror of Faith* no. 107).

Perfect contemplation and the fullness of vision are also union with God. The love by which God loves us cannot be anything outside himself, but it is his own Love and goodness, that is, the Holy Spirit who proceeds from Father and Son and who "unites us to God and God to us" (*On Contemplating God* no. 11). Since the Holy Spirit is the consubstantial Love who unites the Father and the Son, when the Spirit comes into our hearts God loves himself in us. This union is nothing other than the very unity of the Trinity insofar as humans can participate in it — a beatifying union of love. Referring to Matthew 11:27, the abbot says:

> ...just as for the Father to know the Son is nothing else than being what the Son is and for the Son to know the Father is nothing else but being what the Father is..., and just as for the Holy Spirit knowing or comprehending the Father and the Son is being what they are, so too for us created in your image...to love and to fear God and to obey his commands is nothing else but to be and to be one spirit with him. (*On Contemplating God* no. 11)

That William should conceive of one spirit with God as the perfect form of our regaining the lost likeness to God demonstrates the full coherence between his anthropology centered on likeness and his mystical teaching. Our union with God takes place on the level of person, that is, in the person of the Holy Spirit who is the bond uniting Father and Son. Yet we are always God by grace, not by nature.

The Role of the Spirit in the Trinity and the Mystical Life

As we have seen, William's Spirit-centered mysticism concentrates on the Holy Spirit's role as the divine unity. The Holy Spirit is not one *with* the Father and the Son as much as he *is their oneness*. This understanding of the Holy Spirit as

the community of the entire Trinity, a community communicated to humanity in the one spirit with God, is the heart of
the abbot's Spirit-centered mysticism. For William, the ascent
to God begins with our contact with the Incarnate Word and
tends toward union with all three persons by means of the
unifying action of the Spirit. The Word made flesh reveals
the central mystery of God so that we can begin to appropriate it by faith, but it is only by the action of the Holy
Spirit in our hearts that we are drawn up into the mystery
itself. As we have seen, William teaches that the mutuality
of knowing and seeing between the Father and the Son, *precisely as shared*, is the Holy Spirit. This is what it means to
be the Spirit, just as the definition of Bride is to be in love.
So the intersubjective union of the human with God must
be the Spirit's work — this is what the Spirit is and does.

CONCLUSION

William of St. Thierry is one of the true giants of the monastic mystical tradition. Profoundly suspicious of the role of
unaided reason in the task of theology as he was, William displays a speculative power of mind unmatched by any mystic
of his time, especially in his analysis of the relation of love and
understanding in the mystical path and in his understanding
of the role of the Holy Spirit as our union with God. Like
Bernard and the other Cistercians, he put love at the center
of his consideration, especially the notion of the ordering of
love. His conception of this ordering of love, however, was
not so much concerned with explaining the effects of the
ordering process itself as understanding how such ordering

is rooted in our experience of the Trinity through the Holy Spirit.

William's natural gifts for loving passionately come through in his texts, even those that reveal his speculative mind at work. William tends to dwell on the positive aspects of the pursuit of God, the gradual illumination of the intellect, and the increasing fervor of love's flame within the soul. This is why he found the Song of Songs to be the mystical book par excellence. In it he found a rich store of positive images for love, possession, vision, and enjoyment. We conclude with a text from the *Golden Letter:*

> To see the good things of the Lord is to love them, but to love them is to possess them. Let us make every effort to see as much as we are able, so that seeing we may understand, and understanding we may love, and loving we may possess. (*Golden Letter* no. 194)

SUGGESTIONS FOR FURTHER READING

Most of William's mystical writings are available in translations from Cistercian Publications of Kalamazoo, Michigan. The most important of these are the *Exposition on the Song of Songs,* translated by Columba Hart (1970); *The Golden Epistle,* translated by Theodore Berkeley (1971); *The Enigma of Faith,* translated by John D. Anderson (1974); and *The Mirror of Faith,* translated by Thomas X. Davis (1979). For a handy anthology of William's writings, see *William of Saint Thierry: The Way to Divine Union: Selected Spiritual Writings,* edited by M. Basil Pennington (Hyde Park, N.Y.: New City Press, 1998). The best introduction to William's mysticism is David N. Bell, *The Image and Likeness: The Augustinian Spirituality of William of St. Thierry* (Kalamazoo, Mich.: Cistercian Publications, 1984). See also the collected papers of Odo Brooke, *Studies in Monastic Theology* (Kalamazoo, Mich.: Cistercian Publications, 1980).

Two Concluding Prayers

All the mystics presented here had only one reason for writing: to communicate to their contemporaries and to us, their successors, the message that God is near us, indeed, in our very midst. If we turn our attention toward God, if we call upon all our inner resources, God will reveal to us the divine presence in ways that can neither be imagined nor adequately described. Since both knowing and loving are needed for the mystical quest, we would like to close by citing two prayers from mystics treated in this book, one that emphasizes the need for the illumination of our knowing; another that stresses the ordering of love through the action of the Holy Spirit poured out in our hearts:

John the Scot
A Prayer for Illumination

God, our salvation and redemption, You who gave us nature, also bestow grace. Stretch forth your light to those who grope in the shadows of ignorance as they seek You. Call us back from our errors. Hold out your right hand to us who are so weak that we cannot come to You without your aid. Reveal Yourself to those who seek for nothing but You. Shatter the clouds of empty images that prevent the mind's insight from gazing upon You in the way in which You allow Yourself, though invisible, to be seen by those who desire to behold your face, which is their resting place, their final goal, beyond which they desire nothing, because there is nothing beyond the superessential and supreme Good.   — *Periphyseon 3*

WILLIAM OF ST. THIERRY
A Prayer for Ordering Love

O God, Love, Holy Spirit, Love of the Father and the Son
and their substantial Will, dwell in us and set us in order so
that your will may be done in us. Let your will be our will,
so that being ready to do the will of the Lord our God, we
may find his law and his order in the midst of our heart.
Enlighten the eyes of our heart so that we may gaze upon the
unchanging light of your Truth and the form of our mutability
and the changeful inconstancy of our will may be corrected.
May your Bride, our soul, by loving You come to understand
in your love what she is called to do with herself. Rather, by
your dwelling in her, You, the God who is himself your Love
in her, bring it to pass in her that she may love You from your
very Self, O You who are her Love! May You Yourself in her,
love Yourself through her, and in her and through her may
You cause and order all things according to your very Self.

— *Exposition on the Song of Songs* no. 131

THE PRESENCE OF GOD SERIES
BERNARD McGINN

  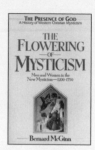

In 1982, Bernard McGinn approached The Crossroad Publishing Company with the idea for a multivolume work on the history of Christian mysticism, from the time of Jesus to the present day. The series that has resulted is the most widely-read, comprehensive, and respected history of Christian mysticism in English, acclaimed by scholars around the world as "classic", "brilliant", and "monumental". We proudly offer the first three volumes of McGinn's series, as follows:

THE FOUNDATIONS OF MYSTICISM
Origins to the Fifth Century

0-8245-1404-1 $29.95 paperback

THE GROWTH OF MYSTICISM
Gregory the Great Through the Twelfth Century

0-8245-1628-1 $29.95 paperback

THE FLOWERING OF MYSTICISM
Men and Women in the New Mysticism 1200-1350

0-8245-1743-1 $39.95 paperback
0-8245-1742-2 $60.00 hardcover

Please support your local bookstore, or call 1-800-707-0670.

For a free catalog, please write us at:
The Crossroad Publishing Co.
481 Eighth Avenue, Suite 1550, New York, NY 10001
Please visit our website at www.crossroadpublishing.com

All prices subject to change.